Seasons of Grace

Wisdom from the Cloister

Mother Gail Fitzpatrick, OCSO

ACTA
ASSISTING CHRISTIANS TO ACT
PUBLICATIONS

Seasons of Grace
Wisdom from the Cloister
by Mother Gail Fitzpatrick, OCSO

Gail Fitzpatrick has been a Trappistine nun for over 40 years and the abbess of Our Lady of the Mississippi Abbey in Dubuque, Iowa for 18 years. Mother Gail is also leading an international effort to build a new monastery, Tautra Mariakloster, near Trondheim in mid-Norway, close to the site of the ruins of an ancient Cistercian monastery. All royalties from the sale of this book will be used for the building of a permanent monastery for the Sisters there.

Edited by Gregory F. Augustine Pierce
Cover design by Tom A. Wright
Cover photo by Bill Witt
Author photo by Sr. Ciaran Shields, OCSO
Page design and typesetting by Barbara Garrison

Copyright © 2000 by Gail Fitzpatrick
Published by ACTA Publications, 4848 N. Clark Street, Chicago, IL 60640-4711, 773-271-1030.

Library of Congress Catalog Number: 00-106104
ISBN: 0-87946-216-7
Year: 05 04 03 02 01 Printing 7 6 5 4 3 2 1
Printed in the United States of America

CONTENTS

To my parents
and to all the wonderful
teachers-in-Christ
who have blessed my life.

FOREWORD

Seasons of Grace might be seen as a monastic retreat that we can hold in our hands. It is not a theological treatise but a reflection on the lived experience of faith, shared hospitably with us as if we were guests at Our Lady of the Mississippi Abbey itself. And it offers the reader a glimpse into an element of monastic life that guests do not often witness—the "chapter talks," also known as "conferences," that the abbess gives to the community on Sundays and principal feast days throughout the year.

These presentations, generally brief and based on the communal experience of the cloistered nuns, have been a vital component of the Christian monastic tradition for some 1700 years and are a link with monasticism's origins as a lay movement within the church. In today's highly competitive and hyper-individualized culture, they serve to remind us of the value of communal wisdom, the sort of wisdom that is nurtured in a community of faith, which in turn strengthens its members to be a sign of hope for others.

One of the things that sets monastic life apart is the opportunity it affords to connect with the Bible on a daily, even hourly, basis—not only in private prayer and reflection but in a community context. In all of the hoopla surrounding the recent rediscovery of women mystics of the monastic tradition—Hildegard of Bingen, for example, now rating her own well-stocked section in the largest music stores—little attention has been paid to the communal nature of their lives. But the poetry and music of Hildegard grew out of her life within a monastery and served a liturgical purpose there. In this little book by Mother Gail Fitzpatrick, the reader comes to see how basic Christian wisdom is engendered within such a community today, making such seemingly abstract notions as the Incarnation or events in the liturgical year come alive for those who—to paraphrase Mother Gail—are willing to let the mystery touch them, here and now.

Monastic people sometimes describe their life as an immersion in Scripture, and I believe that it is this daily fidelity to listening to and reflecting on the Bible that gives monasticism its vitality and makes it appealing to such a wide variety of contemporary seekers—from parish priests to Protestant pastors, from faithful Christians to those who are deeply distrustful of the Bible and the religion it represents.

Entering a monastery is like entering a poem. You find that the practitioners are not trying to convert you to their own point of view but rather are offering you an experience based on the words of psalms and hymnody. As you take in these words, they begin to resonate with your own life—opening doors and changing perceptions. The unaccustomed silence surrounding the words allows their meaning to penetrate in surprising but fruitful ways, until life itself seems to slow down and you feel as if there is all the time in the world to sort things out. It's no wonder that monastery guest houses like the one at Mississippi Abbey are often fully booked months in advance.

"Before Christ comes to us in glory," Mother Gail states, "he will come to us in every moment of our existence." In this book she engages the reader to understand how this might be true—not only for Mother Gail but for the women of her community and for Christians like ourselves. Her reflections remind us that religious faith is meant to fully engage with our lives, even in the midst of suffering and change and loss of hope. As on a retreat, we begin to pare down and simplify and comprehend more clearly that our true task in life is not to do or gain or even understand more but to see and love what is set before us as God's gift and challenge to us.

Kathleen Norris
March 25, 2000
Feast of the Annunciation

INTRODUCTION

The seasons of the Spirit are reflective of the seasons of the year. Here in Iowa, on the bluffs of the Mississippi River, we know well the ecstatic new life of spring, the lush fruitfulness of summer, the melancholy beauty of fall, the stark silence of winter. The cloistered life roots us in one place, and this stability permits us to experience deeply the drama of the alternations both of the physical world around us and of the spiritual life within us.

For example, each winter we can gaze with awe on a frozen landscape or feel the exhilaration of subzero cold on our faces. Likewise, we can experience both the chill that can cover our inner hearts as well as the enrapturing joy we can find in seemingly insignificant moments.

At times, our sense at the Abbey of being truly alive in Christ is overwhelming and clearly urges us on to fidelity in prayer and community service. Then there are other times when there seems to be no meaning or value in anything we do.

In monastic life—as in the lives of all Christians—these alternations of darkness and light, of doubt and clarity, of questioning and contentment are springboards to faith and to to-

11

tal trust in God. However, we usually know that only later, after the fact.

When Saint Paul tells his friends in Corinth that God bestows great encouragement on him in order that he may encourage them, he touches on what I consider the primary call of monastic leaders: to encourage the brothers and sisters. Not just those few who are part of our specific communities, but the entire body of Christ. As Paul puts it:

> Blessed be the God and Father of our Lord Jesus Christ, the merciful Father and the God who gives every possible encouragement; he supports us in any hardship, so that we are able to come to the support of others in every hardship of theirs because of the encouragement that we ourselves receive from God. For just as the sufferings of Christ overflow into our lives, so too does the encouragement we receive through Christ. So if we have hardships to undergo, this will contribute to your encouragement and your salvation; if we receive encouragement, this is to gain for you the encouragement which enables you to bear with perseverance the same sufferings we do.
>
> 2 Corinthians 1:3-6 NJB

The daily or weekly "chapter talks" of the abbot or abbess in a monastery remain the traditional way in which this encouragement is shared with the community. The chapter talk takes its name from the room in the monastery–the Chapter Room–where the community gathers to listen to a chapter of the Rule of St. Benedict. The abbot or abbess then comments on the Rule, or—as in the reflections in this book—on a reading from the liturgy for the day.

The seasons of life, the seasons of the year, and the liturgical seasons are all seasons of grace. I try to stress this in my chapter talks with my Sisters here at Mississippi Abbey and encourage them to look at and embrace each season as it unfolds in their lives as a special grace from God.

These talks have been given over the eighteen years of my abbatial service, and they form the basis for the reflections that I now share with you. They are loosely organized into four parts–Spring, Summer, Fall, and Winter–based on their themes, but you are free to start the book anywhere and proceed in any direction. Let the Spirit move you.

If you ever want to experience the robust seasons in Iowa in our monastic setting, you are welcome to visit us here at Our Lady of the Mississippi Abbey. If you happen to be traveling in

Europe and would like to experience the seasons in even greater drama, visit our Sisters at our new monastery, Tautra Mariakloster, near Trondheim in mid-Norway. On this beautiful and historic island, the alternations of darkness, light, rain, snow, and sun occur in a matter of minutes, not hours or months! The Sisters who are reestablishing Cistercian life at this ancient monastic site are growing to appreciate the ever-changing seasons there as truly seasons of grace. May you do the same, no matter where you find yourself.

Mother Gail Fitzpatrick, OCSO
May 31, 2000
Feast of the Visitation

Spring

1

THE FIELD OF OUR HEARTS

Be patient, therefore, beloved, until the coming of the Lord. The farmer waits for the precious crop from the earth, being patient with it until it receives the early and the late rains. You also must be patient. Strengthen your hearts, for the coming of the Lord is near.

JAMES 5:7-8

As I grow older, I marvel more and more at the wisdom of Mother Church. The constant cycle of the liturgical seasons has a way of penetrating our very life system. For example, each spring I *feel* the need of Lent, and I sense you do, too. We are ready, even anxious, for this time of simplification of externals and intensification of prayer in order to enter more deeply into our own inner heart. There we can be still and simply be with God . . . to allow the Paschal mystery—the mystery of Christ—to touch us.

These thoughts have been going through my mind especially now as the farmers who surround the Abbey are preparing to break the ground with the plow. The plowing of a field is a very apt symbol for the Lenten season and what it is about. You have probably noticed how over the winter the surface of a field becomes, little by little, hard and compacted—almost impenetrable—so that the water tends to run off rather than soak down into the soil. When we get out there and pull a plow through the ground, the plow picks up that surface layer of ground and rolls it over and breaks it up and makes it soft again, so that the soil can receive the moisture and the new seed it needs to be productive once again.

Our lives can be a little like the winter ground. Little by little we can become hard and compacted and almost impenetrable. We can find ourselves living mostly on the surface and not in the deep soil. We need something that will break open the shell of defenses and routine that keep us operating on the surface of existence. We need something that will break us open so that we can get back in touch with the God who dwells in the depths of our heart.

So every spring, the Church says: Come, return to the Lord. Simplify your lives, intensify your desire, allow the Paschal mystery to penetrate every fiber of your being.

How can we go about plowing these depths? How do we break the impenetrable surface of our lives? For one thing, we can look around our lives and see which rows we might plow—down on food here, up on prayer there; down on talking here, up on positive attitude there. We know that these are very little things—they just scratch the surface of our spiritual lives—but at least they show our willingness to enter into the plowing process.

Seasoned farmers know that what they call a "moldboard plow" can have two, three, or even more blades, or "bottoms." To push our analogy, the real work of plowing our spirits is God's work, and during these days of spring God uses the basic two-bottom plow. One of the blades is the events of our daily lives; and the other is the word of God found in the Scriptures. God is working this dual-blade plow in our lives at every moment.

In the time after the Christmas and New Year holidays, it often seems we are riding along lickety-split, bouncing up and down, barely able to hold on to the reins and keep our balance. We just don't have, or take, the time to enter into the depths of life's events, and so we miss many opportunities to experience the divine presence.

Then comes spring and the Lenten season. God takes the reins away from us and says: Slow down; let me get in there and turn things over a bit. Let me uncover for you the hidden meaning of your life.

Maybe you are experiencing loneliness or failure or frustration with others. Perhaps your prayer lacks enthusiasm. Or maybe things are going great. Perhaps you have discovered some new and deep peace, or experienced joy in some job that is going particularly well. It is not enough simply to accept these situations on the surface. We need to let God take them and use them to open up our inner being.

It's the same with the word of God, the second blade on our moldboard plow. During these days of spring, the Scriptures take on very great significance. The readings of each day's liturgy, our personal Bible reading, and our other spiritual reading all hold a message that can cut right through the sod and reveal the rich furrows of our heart. The readings challenge us, stir up our love, unite us with Christ the Word.

Why do we need all this plowing? Simply so that we may enter more deeply into the death of Christ in order to rise to new life in him. Jesus' heart has been broken open on Calvary, and daily in the Eucharist Christ offers himself to us saying: This is my body, which has been *broken for you.*

God, the Good Farmer, during these days of Lent may we allow you to do your work. When we experience something "breaking up our world," instead of trying to avoid it as we usually do, let us take the experience and offer it to you, saying, "Father, use this to open me up and bring forth new life."

2

TO DENY OUR VERY SELVES

"If any want to become my followers, let them deny themselves and take up their cross, and follow me."

MARK 8:34

History tells us of great leaders whose ability to inspire others to heroism was spectacular. They did not promise pleasure and ease but rather hardship for a higher cause. For example, Giuseppe Garibaldi, the great Italian patriot, appealed for recruits in these terms: "I offer neither pay, nor quarters, nor provisions; I offer hunger, thirst, forced marches, battles and death. Let him who loves his country in his heart, and not with his lips only, follow me."

And in the darkest days of the Second World War, Winston Churchill offered his fellow citizens nothing but "blood, toil, tears and sweat."

But no leader surpassed Jesus in the realism and personal candor with which he called those who would follow him: If we wish to follow him, we must deny our very selves, take up our own crosses, and follow in his very demanding footsteps!

We have heard these words a thousand times. We've sung them in the liturgy over and over, year after year. How can we really hear what they mean?

There is self-denial that is voluntary. Each one of us has undertaken it to one extent or another. We say no to something we could have had—and very likely enjoyed. Instead, we say yes to our commitments, whatever they may be. For every life calling has a built-in renunciation of other things. Married life and life in community constantly present us with possibilities of denying ourselves.

But there is a denial of self that is involuntary. It is what God simply takes—without asking our permission. Such self-denial may be demanded in any number of ordinary ways—sickness, the necessities of family life, creeping old age, or our own mistakes. This kind of self-denial is harder to accept...and it is also more sure to unite us with God's will.

Voluntary self-denial—the kind that we try to practice during Lent, for example—is important, but only because it prepares us for involuntary self-denial. If I, figuratively or literally, *always* take the best for myself (cutting into the center of the loaf of bread to get the softest piece, for example, or grabbing the juiciest slice of watermelon and leaving the end slices for someone else), then I will most assuredly buckle when God begins to ask me to deny myself much more seriously and at greater cost—especially if I am not given any or much choice in the matter. If I cannot say no to myself on a material level, I will not be able to relinquish myself on a spiritual level.

Meister Eckhart has some profound thoughts relevant to the words of Jesus that we are considering. According to Eckhart, if the word of God is to be born in our souls it can be done only in silence and simplicity. Eckhart uses two German words, one means "*to let be*," that is, to simply surrender to God's will always, and the other means "*to let go*," that is, to become free of all things that are destructive to our inner tranquillity.

This is one way of understanding "to deny our very selves." We have to let go of even our holy ideas and plans, not just our more obviously base thoughts or deeds.

God is beyond human thought. We cannot contain the divine—nor can we determine our own plan of salvation. To attempt to do so causes endless noise within us.

The incident in the Gospel of Mark that precedes these words of the Lord might be a good illustration of this. Saint Peter has just proclaimed Christ as Messiah—a brilliant moment of recognition. And then Jesus levels an injunction of silence to Peter and the apostles. Why?

Jesus knew the hearts of the people around him. Their thoughts were good, even holy, but they were all wrong. Their thoughts about God were too limited, too human. When Jesus began to teach them the truth—that he must suffer and die and be raised on the third day—we know what happened. Peter couldn't let go of *his* idea of the Messiah. According to Mark, Peter began to "rebuke" Jesus, and Jesus had to reprimand him in no uncertain terms: "Get behind me, Satan! For you are setting your mind not on divine things but on human things" (Mark 8:33).

Unlike Peter, we don't have Jesus by our side to knock down our false images, and so he has to do it in other ways. Perhaps the best is to encourage us in our denial of self. If we want to be his followers, then we have to take up the crosses we are given and follow him. Apparently, there is no other way.

So, if we find ourselves unwilling or unable to let go of something (anything) that seems good or sacred or indispensable in life, and yet that thing also is becoming a din in our inner heart, then maybe that is the very thing we are meant to deny ourselves.

Lord Jesus, you ask us to prefer nothing whatever to you. Help us to "let go and let God"–to fall trustingly into the hands of the Father.

3

TEMPTATION

Then Jesus was led up by the Spirit into the wilderness to be tempted by the devil. He fasted forty days and forty nights, and afterwards he was famished. The tempter came and said to him, "If you are the Son of God, command these stones to become loaves of bread." But he answered, "It is written, 'One does not live by bread alone, but by every word that comes from the mouth of God.'"

MATTHEW 4:1-4

Remember, Moses lived for forty years in Midian before he even had a thought of returning to Egypt to lead the Exodus. He was living simply, caring for sheep on the side of a mountain. I believe that these years of simple labor were purifying him to become a leader of God's people. Only when he was ready did he encounter the burning bush—the symbol of Yahweh—on the holy ground of Mt. Horeb.

In this reading from the Gospel of Matthew, we are again on holy ground, but instead of Mt. Horeb it is a Judean desert, and we're there with the new Moses, Jesus. And like Moses, Jesus is also being purified during his forty days and nights of fasting and prayer in the desert. At the end of this purification, Jesus encounters not Yahweh in a burning bush but Satan. To become not only a leader but the ultimate savior of his people, Jesus has to encounter and confront what every human person must meet in her or his life—evil. And, like us, he has to choose.

The account of Jesus' temptation holds a deep truth for us today. Jesus, the Son of God, shows us how a human being can resist the evil that constantly assaults us and our brothers and sisters all over the world. We have all read commentaries, listened to homilies, and meditated on the temptations of Christ many times. We know that these encounters between Satan and Jesus are like a three-act morality play on how evil creeps into all our lives. We are also aware that by his response Jesus reveals the three things that are most helpful in resisting evil: the word of God, the acceptance of God's will in our lives, and the true worship of God.

The power of our liturgical cycle, when we celebrate the events of our salvation history year after year, lies in the fact that we enter into the celebration from a different place each year. As we reflect on the temptations of Christ each spring, we are always in a place in our lives we have never been before. Our experience of evil in our own hearts and in the world all around us is different each year—perhaps deeper, perhaps more keen than ever before.

We also bring new insights each year into the wonder and power of love and truth and beauty. For example, the story of the temptations came alive for me in a new way in an article by André Chouraqui.[1] His most prominent insight is that the particular passages from the Psalms that Jesus uses to respond to Satan are basically those of the poor but faithful one, the just one, the oppressed one in the face of the enemy (who is none other than Satan himself). Chouraqui points out that the innocent one—Jesus—has only one weapon with which to withstand the evil: his voice. His hands are empty; God alone is his weapon; his trust in God is absolute. It makes a difference to pray the Psalms with this in mind.

In listening to the story of the temptations of Jesus, it is helpful to bring to our reflection our most pressing temptation and how we are facing it. Jesus means for us to learn from him how to throw our care on God and then to stand firm and wait.

Lord, in you alone I want to put my trust. Be my one weapon against every temptation.

4

KNOWN BY GOD

*O L*ORD*, you have searched me and
known me.*

To be known, truly known, can be the most
joyous, exhilarating experience of a person's life.
It can also be the most frightening. Most, if not
all, of us at sometime have suffered from this
fear: If my family, my friends, my colleagues really knew my most secret thoughts and desires,
they wouldn't love me.

Jesus seemed to understand this deep human longing to be known, accepted, loved...and
so he stressed it more than once. I know whom
I have chosen, he seemed to say. My sheep have
only to hear my voice, and they will follow me.

Psalm 139 is one that has always been a great comfort to me personally. I say it whenever life is a bit less than enchanting—so I say it fairly often! "O LORD, you have searched me and known me. You know when I sit down and when I rise up....Even before ever a word is on my tongue, O LORD you know it completely....Such knowledge is too wonderful for me; it is so high I cannot attain it."

I always say this psalm when I am in a plane racing down the runway for takeoff. "If I take the wings of the morning and settle at the farthest limits of the sea, even there your hand shall lead me, and your right hand shall hold me fast."

I had always understood this psalm as an outburst of joy in the Lord's constant presence and knowledge of his people. Recently, however, I've come to understand that it is much more than that. It is also an expression of dread and fear at what it means to be known by God.

When the psalmist says, "You hem me in behind and before, and lay your hand upon me," he or she is in fact complaining: God, you're too close. I want to escape from your presence, but I can't. Even when I think I am covered in darkness the very darkness is light to you.

The poet continues, "You have *searched* me," not "You have searched *for* me" or not even "You have searched for *me*." God *searches* us—

digging into us like someone searching for buried treasure. God's knowledge of us can be too much for us. But then, at the very end of the psalm, the psalmist yields again to the blessing of being known: "Search me, O God, and know my heart. Test me and know my thoughts."

God searches us—not once and for all but over and over—and this is both our joy and pain. God knows us so intimately—in our weakness and also in our potential—that we are never left alone, even when we want to be. We are always being recreated, drawn to new life.

In Saint John's vision of a new heaven and a new earth in the Book of Revelation, God dwells with the people, wiping every tear from their eyes, promising no more death, no more mourning, no more pain: "See, I am making all things new" (Revelation 21:5).

In the spring, every particle of nature seems to cry out in newness of life. Behold! God is making *all things* new. We can practically see in the blossoms and fresh green grass and hear in the chirping of the birds the fulfillment of Saint Paul's promise to the Romans: "The creation waits with eager longing for the revealing of the children of God" (Romans 8:19). We ourselves—walking with Christ through the Paschal Mystery—also feel alive in a new way in springtime.

Yet still we have a bit of Nicodemus in us. We want to ask the Lord: What is this new life that you talk about? What really does it mean to be born again? What does the exhilaration of a beautiful spring day or the joy of loving companionship have to do with taking up a cross?

The new life that we have been given is simple. It is this moment and the freedom by which we live this moment. Each succeeding moment is fresh, genuinely new, not a rerun. All we need do to enter into our new life is to be fully present, open and listening. Then the creative Spirit is free to search us.

Father , we pray that we will yield ourselves to this new life at each moment as we experience the joy and challenge of being known intimately by you.

5

ROOTS

"Abide in me, as I abide in you. Just as a branch cannot bear fruit by itself unless it abides in the vine, neither can you unless you abide in me. I am the vine, you are the branches. Those who abide in me and I in them, bear much fruit, because apart from me you can do nothing."

JOHN 15:4-5

People react differently to change. Some dread it, others can't live without frequent changes in all kinds of things in their lives, and still others hit a happy balance between the ability to adapt easily to change and the willingness to be content with a certain routineness or stability in life.

What is it, besides one's innate personality, that permits us to experience serious changes without trauma? I think it has to do with the rootedness we all experience in springtime. In spring, we watch with awe as the small plants the gardeners have been nurturing since winter are transplanted into the warm earth. To survive, these seedlings must have roots. It's the same with us. It is what is deep within us that permits us to move freely and with ease into a new environment, a new home, a new job, a new relationship. If we are deeply rooted, change with growth can occur.

Often we can live through very painful and stretching sorts of changes in our life with a fair amount of ease. After a new plateau of growth has been achieved, we look back with awe and surprise and wonder how we did it.

Our roots as followers of Jesus go deep. The whole Judeo-Christian tradition is behind us. The Scriptures from which we continuously draw life and inspiration don't answer all the questions, but they do give us a basis for living with the absurdities of life. Our sacramental life gives us constant contact with the Risen Christ. Our communal Christian life—whether in monastery or parish—keeps us rooted, perhaps more than we are even aware, to the degree that each one of us has assimilated its spirit and values.

These are our roots. And so, we really have nothing to fear, even if our lives seem to have been turned upside down by change. If I am deeply rooted in Jesus, it really doesn't make too much difference whether I am a doctor, cashier, monk, or mother. My life is deeper than what I do.

And if we simply live the moment at hand—without allowing ourselves to dread the future and without too much attention to the past except for a grateful glance now and then—we can hang loose and let the Lord move us as he will by the breath of his Spirit.

Lord Jesus, you tell us over and over not to be afraid. May we live each moment in deep trust as we abide in you.

6

CAUGHT BY AWE

Jesus said to Simon, "Put out into the deep water and let down your nets for a catch." Simon answered, "Master, we have worked hard all night long but have caught nothing. Yet if you say so, I will let down the nets." When they had done this, they caught so many fish that their nets were beginning to break. So they signaled to their partners in the other boat to come and help them. And they came and filled both boats so that they began to sink. But when Simon Peter saw it, he fell down at Jesus' knees, saying, "Go away from me, Lord, I am a sinful man!" For he and all who were with him were amazed at the catch of fish that they had taken.

Luke 5:4-9

All of us at one time or another have been "caught by awe"—rendered almost speechless by beauty in nature or art or by an overwhelming experience of peace or joy. The experience was so great that we simply didn't want to disturb it with words.

In this story from the Gospel of Luke, Saint Peter is struck by a powerful experience, the experience of deep conversion. Imagine him standing knee-deep in fish, his boat almost sinking from the huge catch that Jesus had produced, right after Peter—professional fisherman that he was—had come back from a night's fishing that had brought in exactly nothing. For a man like Peter, this had to be more amazing than seeing someone walk on water (which, of course, he later did).

Peter does speak, but his words were those of an awe-struck person. In a flash, he realizes that he is in the presence of divine power. The first thing that comes to his mind, however, is his own sinfulness: "Go away from me, Lord, I am a sinful man!"

There is a similar story in the Book of Isaiah (see chapter 6). The prophet sees in a vision the Lord of glory and hears the angels crying out: "Holy is the LORD of hosts." In the face of this divine majesty Isaiah, like Peter, is suddenly aware of his sinfulness: "Woe is me! I am lost, for I am a man of unclean lips, and I live among a people of unclean lips; yet my eyes have seen the King, the LORD of hosts!" But the Seraphim touch his lips with a live coal taken from the altar: "Now that this has touched your lips, your guilt has departed and your sin is blotted out."

It is in the presence of divine majesty that we become aware of the truth about ourselves. This is the root of true conversion. Neither Peter nor Isaiah know enough to say, "Have mercy." Rather, their instinctive shock response is to seek to remove themselves from that presence, which is so glorious, so powerful, so holy that we humans literally cannot stand it. But the Lord, in both instances, carries his beloved through the experience of awe to new life. The Lord does not allow them to wallow in their feelings or to run away because it is too much for them. Instead he calls them more deeply to himself.

Thus the most far reaching and deeply effective conversion takes place not when someone tells us how bad we are, but when someone reveals to us our true goodness and holiness. Only this revelation is powerful enough to draw us into a whole new way of seeing and living "Here am I; send me!" (Isaiah 6:8), says Isaiah. "Do not be afraid," Jesus tells Peter, "from now on you will be catching people" (Luke 5:10).

In an absolute sense, only God can show

us these magnetic qualities in ourselves, and when we glimpse—however briefly—our ultimate holiness, then we have a "theophany," an experience of the divine like the ones Peter and Isaiah had. When we do, our life is totally changed.

We can't make these theophanies happen. They are pure grace. But I believe they occur more than we realize—if we are open to recognizing them. And although we cannot bring them about, either for ourselves or for others, we can let out our nets for a catch—even when we haven't caught a fish all night.

One thing we can do is to come together regularly and speak honestly with one another about the values we share and how we live them. In our very concrete living of the Christian life, it is wise to evaluate the way we live those values with a trusted friend or guide or group on a regular basis. That may sound pretty mechanical, but I believe that such sharing can bring about the kind of awe experienced by Peter and Isaiah.

Part of this sharing process is listening. To really listen to another requires a great deal of self-discipline. We have to put ourselves on a back burner in order to really hear others. As Saint Benedict would say, we have to prefer the good (in this case, the words) of others to our own.

There is power in this kind of exercise. Of course, this listening is a function of silence as well as an activity of speech. Perhaps we will become more truly silent persons as we become better listeners. By truly listening to others, we allow them—paradoxically—to become more silent interiorly, because so often interior noise is caused by, or aggravated by, the frustration of feeling unheard or misunderstood.

Let my interior silence be a net where you can be caught, God. Let my reverent listening allow myself and others to be caught by awe.

7

THE TEARS OF OUR PRAYER

*Create in me a clean heart, O God, and
put a new and right spirit within me.*

PSALM 51:10

Lent is a time that enables us to get down to
essentials, to let what is unimportant or merely a
distraction recede into the background. In the
quiet that follows, we can hear again the primal
call into a loving relationship with God that re-
sults in a special kind of prayer.

"Prayer with tears" or "compunction of heart"
is a way of describing the reality of being touched
or pierced (*punctis*) by the awareness of our true
state before God. This is the mark of true prayer:
tears springing from a heart that is intensely at-
tentive. But compunction does not mean merely
feeling sorrow for personal transgressions.

Saint Benedict understood this kind of prayer to be something far richer. When we are overwhelmed by the love of God who forgives us no matter what we do, we are also touched by an overwhelming desire for separation from sin and inclusion into God's kingdom. This desire, which may last for a moment or for months, may result in tears of joy as well as tears of sorrow.

At the heart of compunction there is a sense of pain. This pain, this inner pricking or even downright puncturing of our heart, is caused by our experience of God's love and our intense desire to return that love. God's love pierces our heart and calls us into union with divinity itself. It is at this moment that we sense in a real way the heaviness and burden of our own sin—probably not a particular sin, although an individual could be made aware of an area in his or her life that has not been open to God's will; but more often it is the overriding sense of our general sluggishness. When we are in this space, we see our compromises for what they are, or rather we feel the effects of our habits of self-indulgence. This can be a moment of intense purification of our heart.

From the first book of Samuel, we know the beautiful story of Hannah, the mother of Samuel, who begged the Lord—with many tears—for a child. And we know the Lord heard her prayer.

There is another scene, maybe less familiar to us, of this same intense prayer with tears. In the book of Isaiah, the king Hezekiah has just received this diagnosis (from the prophet himself): "You shall die, you shall not recover" (Isaiah 38:1). What does Hezekiah do? He turns his face to the wall (which is like entering into the private chamber of one's heart) and prays to Yahweh, shedding many tears. "The word of the LORD came to Isaiah: 'Go and say to Hezekiah, Thus says the LORD, the God of your ancestor David: I have heard your prayer, I have seen your tears; I will add fifteen years to your life'" (Isaiah 38:5).

You might think that these prayers with tears are different from ours. Hannah and Hezekiah were in desperate straits and were praying for a particular favor—in one case, a child, in the other, a cure. Certainly compunction—being directly touched by God's love—*is* a different experience for each of us. But there is a common element. In each instance, whatever it is that prompts the heart, the heart pours itself out in tears and these are heard by God. It isn't that our tears play on God's sympathy. It's rather that the tears themselves cleanse our hearts, purify them, and enable us to receive God's gift—whatever that gift may be.

The tears that accompany the prayer of compunction may not be visible or wipe-able. I think

a heart can weep dry tears. In one sense wet
tears are easier, but I am not advocating that we
induce tears—by onions or any other means! That
would just be a lot of ego playing. But if prayer
with tears is an important element in the Christian tradition, we should try to understand it if
and when this gift is granted to us at any time.
Tears of compunction are not the prerogative of
those of us who are strong "feelers." *All* of us
can be touched in some way by the spirit of
compunction, and we are.

---

*Holy Spirit, draw us more deeply into
the life and love of the Trinity. Open our
hearts to receive you through our tears.*

8

FORGIVENESS

*Jesus said, "Father, forgive them, for they
do not know what they are doing."*

LUKE 24:34

Father Lawrence Jenco, an American Servite
priest, was kidnapped in Lebanon and held for
eight years. At the end of his captivity, a man
named Sayeed, one of the guards who had at
times brutalized him, came to ask Jenco for his
forgiveness. Jenco was overwhelmed and answered: "Sayeed, there were times I hated you. I
was filled with anger and revenge for what you
did to me and my brothers. But Jesus said on a
mountain top that I was not to hate you. I was to
love you. Sayeed, I need to ask God's forgiveness and yours." Jenco felt empowered by this

47

act of forgiveness. He felt free to go back and live a normal life after his liberation. [2]

This account is very striking, but it points to something more important than the act of forgiveness itself, even when terrible offenses occur. It points to what happens *after* the forgiveness. Because he was able to forgive his captors and to ask for forgiveness himself, Father Jenco was able to lead a somewhat normal life from the time he was released until he died recently.

But what happens when we are not able to forgive or to ask for forgiveness?

Memory is a very powerful human capacity. Our memory includes a strong, negative tendency to remember wrongs, unpleasant events, and put-downs. The healing of these memories doesn't mean "forgetting" them. We can't forget deliberately, and sometimes when we try to forget we are really just evading an issue.

Turning negative memories into positive ones comes with seeing everything as coming from God. When, like Fr. Jenco, we can experience even painful occurrences as moments of God's mercy for ourselves and others, then we know we have forgiven and been forgiven. God is Love, but we can only discover that truth through forgiveness.

There can be communal—as well as individual—negative memories that need to be healed. These community memories can hold people back from change and growth. The older of us need to watch that we don't pass on unforgiven resentments and prejudices to new generations.

Forgiveness and reconciliation are not isolated acts that end with themselves. They are like opening up a dam. They empower new life, give fresh hope to others, and release boundless energy.

We don't forget the past. We allow the past—all of it—to be a springboard into the future.

Lord Jesus, heal us and teach us to forgive as you have forgiven.

9

THE CUP

(James and John) said to him, "Grant us to sit one at your right hand and one at your left, in your glory." But Jesus said to them, "You do not know what you are asking. Are you able to drink the cup that I drink, or to be baptized with the baptism that I am baptized with?"

MARK 10:37-38

A young man approaches Jesus with a question. "Good Teacher, what must I do to inherit eternal life?" (Mark 10:17). Shortly thereafter, two disciples come with a different request: "Grant us to sit, one at your right hand and one at your left, in your glory" (Mark 10:37).

To the first young man, Jesus responds with

an invitation that could have changed this person's life radically. But the man recognizes how much he has to leave behind and walks away sad.

To his two young apostles, Jesus responds not with a reprimand for their obvious ambition but with a clear statement of what discipleship means: Can you drink the cup?

In a sense, the young man and the two young followers of Jesus have the same problem: They want to be disciples on their terms. They sense in this "good Master" something very attractive and want to be part of his goodness, but none of them have a clue what Jesus is really about.

"You do not know what you are asking," he tells the sons of Zebedee. They are asking the wrong question, and for Jesus it is really important that we ask the right question.

But even with the wrong question, Jesus draws them into the core of what it means to be a disciple of his: to drink the cup he drinks, to share in his baptism. From our vantage point we know to what that cup and baptism refer. Walking along the dusty road that day, James and John did not.

In quiet prayer, we need to let the question of Jesus dwell in our own heart: Can we drink his cup? Can we be immersed with him in the baptism of pain and suffering for the salvation of the world? Can we go through the terrible experiences that he had to go through? Can we face hatred and death as he has done? Can we sell everything and follow him?

Maybe we can, but questions arise. What is there in most of our lives that remotely resembles the cup of Christ's suffering? How can we glorify our little misunderstandings and frustrations or sense of loneliness or uselessness as anything like the abandonment Jesus experienced?

These are useless questions. Jesus has said to us through the disciples: "The cup that I drink you will drink, and with the baptism with which I am baptized, you will be baptized" (Mark 10:39). Can we believe this promise? Can we give up trying to set our own terms and just try to live fully and consciously as followers of Jesus? Can we believe that by this very act we will be united to his saving love?

We cannot judge our own life experience as worthy or unworthy of Christ. It is not for us to judge ourselves or others. All we need do is believe that once we commit our life to God, all of it becomes acceptable to him. The cup that we drink with Christ is here and now. In accepting the unknown, the disappointments, the dryness, the ordinariness of our life, we are with

Christ—neither on his left nor his right, but with him nonetheless.

Not one moment, not one experience of our life is outside of this promise. It is all part of the Lord's cup, and we *will* drink it.

God, I have committed my life to you, so I trust Christ's cup in my life is in accepting the unknown, the disappointments, the dryness. Jesus promised, "You shall drink my cup." Thank you, Lord.

10

OBEDIENCE

Let the same mind be in you that was in Christ Jesus, who, though he was in the form of God, did not regard equality with God as something to be exploited, but emptied himself, taking the form of a slave, being born in human likeness. And being found in human form, he humbled himself and became obedient to the point of death—even death on a cross.

PHILIPPIANS 2:5-8

Obedience is not an easy or popular topic to talk about. Obedience is never easy, although it may become less problematic if we understand its true nature. Obedience has seldom been popular, although most of us have been taught from a very early age that it is a great value.

I can say in one sentence the main point I want to make in regard to obedience: Obedience is the form love takes. This is the bottom line, the only reality that would motivate me to want to live a life orientated to obedience.

There's a strong theological basis for believing that obedience is the form love takes. It is the life and death of Jesus Christ. What we celebrate in the passion of Christ is that perfect love is the deepest meaning of our existence. Jesus' love was clearly defined. It was a love that gave itself over to the will of his beloved Father. "I have come down from heaven, not to do my own will, but the will of him who sent me" (John 6:38), he said. And again: "My food is to do the will of the one who sent me" (John 4:34). And yet again: "My Father, not what I want but what you want" (Matthew 26:39).

Thus, the love of Jesus for the Father took the form of obedience. Between Jesus and the Father there was a logic of love. Obedience to the will of his Father permeated his life, but his obedience was never cringing. The obedience of Jesus to his Father was—and continues to be— a communion between them. Jesus actually loves the Father's will, and their absolute sharing in the same desire is the salvation of us all.

So it is not problematic to accept the obedience of Jesus as a holy and healthy thing. But what of us? Is Christ's obedience to the Father in any way normative for those of us who are Christians today? I think it is.

In Baptism, we are buried in Christ's death and we rise with him in his resurrection. Saint Paul says we are called as disciples of Christ to have the "mind" of Christ. That means we are called to focus towards God all the energies of our being and to follow Christ in the way of his perfect obedience to the Father's will.

When the disciples asked Jesus to teach them to pray as he did, he gave them a very simple prayer that contains a very basic prescription: "Your will be done" (Matthew 6:10). We Christians are called to learn to listen to the call of God in a way that is analogous to Christ's way. We are to yield in obedience to God's will, recognizing that it is merely the form that love takes.

Jesus, help us to hear the call of God and to obey it out of love, preferring the will of God to our own.

11

FRAGRANCE OF CHRIST

Thanks be to God, who in Christ always leads us in triumphal procession, and through us spreads in every place the fragrance that comes from knowing him. For we are the aroma of Christ to God among those who are being saved and among those who are perishing; to the one a fragrance from death to death, to the other a fragrance from life to life.

2 CORINTHIANS 2:14-16

To God, we are the "fragrance" or "aroma" of Christ, according to Saint Paul. What can this possibly mean? I connect this idea with the story of Isaac. Picture Isaac sitting in his chair, old and feeble, quite blind, as described in Genesis 27. Jacob enters, dressed in Esau's clothes, with ani-

mal skins tied around his own scrawny arms.
Isaac calls him to come close, so he can touch
him and smell him. "Ah, the smell of my son is
like the smell of a field that the Lord has blessed"
(Genesis 27:27), he says. Isaac recognizes his
son by his smell, and likewise the Father smells
the fragrance of his only Son, Christ, in us.

This aroma of ours is constant—not just
when we are good and virtuous, but always. That
is what our Baptism is all about: We have "put
on" Christ, just like Jacob put on animal skins on
his thin limbs. God can "smell" the fragrance of
Christ on us at all times, no matter what we are
doing.

Now, the analogy with Isaac and Jacob limps
because Esau was not a willing participant in
the exchange, as Jesus was and as we should
be. Esau's birthright and blessing were stolen by
fraud. But Christ chose to cover us with his own
flesh; he bought us at the high price of his life.
And we have become, through Baptism and Eucharist, the actual Body of Christ.

Our life as Christians maintains a balance
between believing deeply that we are Christ's
and knowing that Christ is God's. We smell like
Christ to the Father, and that is good. Yet at the
same time we know deep in our hearts that if
we are not to be a fraud we must live more and
more united to Christ. The fragrance of Christ is

already ours, there's no doubt about it, but we must respond to his Spirit within us and act more like him toward our brothers and sisters if we are to justify sharing in his birthright.

We need to live each day trying to become, in our own flesh and blood and personal idiosyncrasies, who we truly are meant to be—God's beloved, the fragrance of his Son.

What dignity is ours!

Yes, Lord Jesus, we are the good odor of your anointing. May we be broken open so that the whole world may be filled with its fragrance.

12

THE PATH JESUS TOOK

Then he began to teach them that the Son of Man must undergo great suffering, and be rejected by the elders, the chief priests and the scribes, and be killed, and after three days rise again....Peter took him aside and began to rebuke him. But turning and looking at his disciples, he rebuked Peter and said, "Get behind me Satan! For you are setting your mind not on divine things but on human things."

MARK 8:31-33

This gospel passage brings us face to face with the rejected cross, the shameful cross, the cross of which Saint Peter wants no part—not for himself and not for the Master. (It is interesting that the cross was not used as a Christian symbol until about three centuries after Jesus' death. So the embarrassment felt by the early Church is deep-seated.)

Peter's rejection of the cross holds meaning for us. First, it indicates in a negative sort of way that Peter was not aware that his own destiny was bound up with this young rabbi with whom he had been traveling for a year or maybe a little longer. Peter was smart enough to see that if Jesus was serious about receiving total rejection from the Jewish authorities, this is very bad news for himself as well. So "the Rock" did what most of us would do, he denied the bad news immediately and unequivocally.

This leads to a second important lesson for us. Peter's response was to trust his own human reason over the wisdom of God. As Saint Paul later said to the Corinthians: To the Jews, the cross is an obstacle they cannot get over; to the Gentiles, the cross is pure foolishness.

Then Jesus looked at *all* of the disciples (because he knew that Peter spoke the thoughts of them all) and rejected their feeble attempts to talk him out of his destiny. Just as he did when he was tempted in the desert with other visions of salvation, Jesus saw the real evil in Peter's solicitous advice, and he called it by its real name: "Get behind me, Satan!"

Why was Jesus so harsh? So uncompromising? So condemning? Didn't he understand that Peter was just being human in his fear and lack of understanding?

Jesus perceived that Peter was tempting him to try to alter God's will, and *that* is what the devil truly does.

Somehow, Jesus knew that he *must* suffer. How he came to realize this is probably beyond our understanding, but it is clear that Jesus was convinced that this had to happen (and of course in retrospect he was right). After his resurrection Jesus taught the two disciples walking to Emmaus: "Was it not necessary that the Messiah should suffer these things and then enter into his glory?" (Luke 24:26). Once Jesus came to believe that he had to suffer, therefore, to deviate from the path he was on would have been to go contrary to the mission the Father had entrusted to him. The passion of Jesus was not a quirk of fate. It was a necessity.

Sometimes in our own lives we know with deep conviction that we *must* suffer this or that personal difficulty or trial. Often this knowledge comes only later; after the suffering is over. Nevertheless, it is a very precious insight when we can say of the painful events of life: It was necessary. This insight allows us to become reconciled totally with the will of God.

This incident in the Gospel is terribly important for us as individuals in our own life of discipleship of Christ. We also *must* walk the path Jesus took. We cannot allow human esteem, popularity, power, love of ease and comfort, or selfishness in any form to dominate our lives. Those values are opposed to what Jesus stood for.

Repentance is about turning away from one set of values and accepting another. Peter repented not once, but many times, and in the end he walked right behind his Master to the cross. When Jesus hung on a cross, it brought the whole world to one decision: Are you for him or against him? It's a choice we Christians make over and over again.

Saint Benedict says to prefer nothing whatever to Christ. Repent today: Choose Christ.

Crucified Jesus, help us to walk with you, even when our human nature shrinks from the cross and wants to reject it. Help us to trust that the Father knows what is necessary.

13

EMPTY AT EASTER

We have this treasure in clay jars, so that it may be made clear that this extraordinary power belongs to God and does not come from us.

2 Corinthians 4:7

We should all feel very humble before the primary mystery of our faith: the resurrection. It is a gift that we don't want to take for granted. There are two aspects of the resurrection that are important for us to remember and to believe are pure gift.

First, we hold the gift of Christ's resurrection in vessels of clay—our very bodies. Second, it is the resurrection that created our community–and still does.

During his lifetime, Jesus met and touched many people. Many apparently believed in his goodness and extraordinary power, but only a relatively small number made any radical change in their lifestyle to show their allegiance to him.

After Jesus rose from the dead, however, a whole new community of believers came forth. It wasn't just that people changed their minds or finally made a decision to follow Jesus. It was that somehow they experienced him as actually in their midst, and they celebrated this and made it happen by breaking bread together. By his living Spirit, a diverse group of people became a new living body. They became what we are still today, the Body of Christ.

So during these final days of Spring, we live through and re-live not only what happened to Jesus but what has happened—and continues to happen—to us as well. As Saint Paul put it, "We are...always carrying in the body the death of Jesus, so that the life of Jesus may also be made visible in our bodies" (2 Corinthians 4:10) and "...so that, just as Christ was raised from the dead by the glory of the Father, so we too might walk in newness of life" (Romans 6:4).

Saint Augustine said that the Eucharist is *our own mystery*. By that I think he meant that it is *we* who have been brought from death to life, *we* who have been molded into a community of believers.

We carry the glory of the risen Christ in vessels made of earth itself—that is, in our bodies. Some of those vessels are large and sturdy, others are slender and fragile; some are beautifully enameled, others are funny looking. We are a bunch of clay jars, walking around and carrying a treasure that is beyond imagination within us.

Often I don't feel very fervent during Lent. I don't fast well, or pray well, or read well. My own "clay jar" feels weak and cracked. So by the time we get to the special liturgies of Holy Thursday, Good Friday, and Holy Saturday, I don't feel ready for Easter. I want an extra week to prepare my clay jar to be worthy of Easter.

But the power of the resurrection isn't dependent on my strength or fervor or readiness. All God requires is an empty vessel. The Spirit of the risen Jesus lives in our very bodies. The power of God catches us in our very weakness. By his resurrection, Jesus has created a community of clay pots, each filled with the seeds of eternal glory.

Lord, grant us eyes to see that we are full of the beginning of your glory.

Summer

14

THE HEART OF GRATITUDE

"...that the world may know that you have sent me and have loved them even as you have loved me."

JOHN 17:23

For a long time, I have had this thought: The contemplative is "one who weeps"—for his or her own sin and suffering and for the sin and suffering of every single person in the history of the world. The central job of all contemplatives is to stand—poor, naked, and powerless—before God and to weep because human beings are capable of wounding the very heart of the Son of God.

What this means, I think, is that human beings are capable of blocking the loving mercy that flows from the heart of Jesus. But how do we do that? We know it does not happen because of our human weakness, our faults, or our failures. God certainly can handle those. If not these, however, then what in us can possibly obstruct God's love? I believe it is despair, because despair is the only sin that can truly blind us to the love and mercy of God.

There is an attitude today that is not uncommon. Many people feel that things in their lives are hopeless, that there isn't much to live for, that no one cares about them or their problems. (The rise in suicide among the young, the explosion in the number of people suffering clinical depression, the growing number of incidents of euthanasia and physician-assisted suicide among the sick and elderly are all signs of this.)

The love of God, flowing from the pierced heart of Jesus Christ, is always there for us, but despair causes us to block it from our own lives. So anyone who comprehends the depth of the love God has for every person, *must* weep and pray.

There's more to it, though. Despair comes not at the beginning but at the end of a long and painful road. In a revelation to Saint Margaret Mary Alacoque in 1674, Jesus said it is *ingratitude* that offends him most deeply, and I believe he said this because he recognized that ingratitude is the first step on the path to despair.

Each one of us in our experience on the human level has at times gone out of our way to be kind or helpful or thoughtful to another and been met with ingratitude. It hurt, and often it caused us to withdraw. There wasn't necessarily an overt rebuff or intentional meanness on the other person's part, but simply a lack of any response that would have acknowledged our gift of self.

Thus is the cycle of love blocked. If we, whose gifts are often tinged with some degree of self-seeking, can feel the hurt of ingratitude, what about God, whose gift is total and pure love? In the divine scale of things, however, what ingratitude does to God is not that important; God's love continues to pour out. It is what ingratitude does to us that is the problem. Gratitude is what opens our hearts to receive God's mercy, and by not receiving with gratitude the gift of redeeming love we choose to live in the hell of our own selfishness.

"Do you at least give me consolation by making up for their ingratitude as far as you are able," the vision of the Sacred Heart of Jesus told Margaret Mary.[3] That is the task of those who weep.

Even on a psychological level, gratitude is the mark of an essentially healthy person. To accept the self is to come to love the battles fought, the wounds sustained, to be grateful for everything that has made us *who* and *what* we are. This means that if we are to be whole persons, free and capable of true love, we have to kiss the wounds that have forced us to stretch beyond ourselves. I don't mean this in a masochistic sense of a person constantly reliving hurts, conjuring up painful situations over and over. But gratitude means looking with wonder and reverence on *all* that has made us what we are today.

We have to accept every event and person in our life, to forgive those who hurt us, to bless those who love us. We have to believe that we are who we are not *in spite* of the pain and frustrations in our life, but *because* of them. Then and only then can we let go of painful situations or relationships. Otherwise they hang like weights around our neck. Remember the words of the psalmist: "I praise you, for I am fearfully and wonderfully made" (Psalm 139:14).

Spiritual health and holiness and psychological health and wholeness go hand in hand. If we can say "Thank You, God" for our life *in its entirety*, then the spiritual and psychological are truly integrated. (But we have to mean it!)

And if we are successful, where does that leave those who weep? Well, there is such a thing as weeping for joy. Perhaps we should be weeping from a sense of overwhelming gratitude for the gift of love and mercy poured out in the wounded heart of Jesus.

Father, you created all things good and never stop delighting in your work. Help me to see the world through your eyes and to receive with gratitude all that comes to me through the loving heart of your Son.

15

SIMPLICITY OF LIFE

*"Take nothing for your journey, no staff,
nor bag, nor bread, nor money–not
even an extra tunic."*

LUKE 9:3

"Simplicity of life" means different things to
different people, depending on the context in
which they operate. For instance, a suburban
family with multiple responsibilities in the civic,
social, religious, and political spheres of their
life might escape to the country for a few weeks
during the summer "to live a simple life" close to
nature. This vacation does not necessarily mean
they are without basic conveniences, but simplicity to them means living without the pres-
sure of many demands and involvements.

Scientists or scholars may, at the price of financial advancement, dedicate their entire lives to a particular study or investigation. It might be said of such people that they live a simple life even amid their normal activity, because all their activity is disciplined and directed, focused toward a single end.

A combination of both of these examples can help us appreciate simplicity of life. Simplicity of life is—simply—a life that is trimmed down radically. Unnecessary involvements and luxuries are trimmed off, so that life can have minimal pressures. At the same time, life is freed—through personal and communal discipline—toward a single end.

It is not possible to attain simplicity of life totally through external structures, including the monastic life. A lot depends on our personal desire and willingness to make choices that free us. We have to look critically at what we call our "needs." Simplicity of life demands an ability to be content with little rather than more, and this is where we feel the crunch, even in the cloister.

Still, the ideal of simplicity of life is greatly attractive, and where we live it deeply we experience real joy and contentment. The greatest enemy to this ideal is within ourselves: a lack of the personal discipline that embodies total singleness of purpose and the radical sharing of ourselves and things.

Less is better than more, little is better than a lot. We can find deep joy in not hoarding for a rainy day, in sharing our gifts, ideas, and even our faults and weaknesses. Simplicity of living brings joy, because it is the complete throwing in of our lot with the Christian community.

Lord of simplicity, free us from always needing more, and teach us to be content and to share, since all that comes from you is gift.

16

RECEIVE GOD WELL

He entered Jericho and was passing through it. A man was there named Zacchaeus; he was a chief tax collector and was rich. He was trying to see who Jesus was, but on account of the crowd he could not, because he was short in stature. So he ran ahead and climbed a sycamore tree to see him, because he was going to pass that way. When Jesus came to the place, he looked up and said to him, "Zacchaeus, hurry and come down; for I must stay at your house today." So he hurried down and was happy to welcome him. All who saw it began to grumble and said, "He has gone to be the guest of one who is a sinner." Zacchaeus stood there and said to the Lord, "Look, half of my possessions, Lord, I will give to the poor; and if I have

defrauded anyone of anything, I will
pay back four times as much." Then
Jesus said to him, "Today salvation has
come to this house."

LUKE 19:1-9

In the familiar and very loved gospel story of Zacchaeus, who was a tax collector and who welcomed Jesus into his home, we find an apprenticeship of charity, a school of love—especially love of God.

In this story there is a big surprise. We would have expected that Zacchaeus, being a smart man, a man of means, someone who knew how to seize an opportunity, would have found a way to meet the Lord and invite him to his house for a meal. The surprise is that Jesus doesn't wait for Zacchaeus to make a move. He calls Zacchaeus out of the sycamore tree and invites himself into Zacchaeus' house.

Jesus acts with us as he did with Zacchaeus. He invites himself into our hearts as well, without waiting for us to make the first move. He takes the initiative and says: I and the Father will come to you and we will make our home with you.

Thus does God come to dwell within us! This isn't pious fantasy; it is reality. God is already dwelling within us. But are we always aware of that presence? When Zacchaeus received Jesus into his house he received salvation: "Today salvation has come to this house."

How do we experience the God within? Is it as mercy that covers our sins, much like a wave covering a sandbar as the tide advances? Is it as a stillness that in the midst of turmoil draws us into its center? Is it as fire that empowers us to go on loving, even when things seem pretty hopeless? Is it as wisdom that grants us insight into the mystery that is life?

This day salvation, mercy, stillness, fire, wisdom have come to our house. Let us receive God as Zacchaeus did, with humility and a willingness to change our lives.

O marvel! You, Lord, come to my house even before I think to ask. In that awareness let me lovingly honor you by continuing to cherish every manifestation of your presence.

17

PROPHETS IN OUR MIDST

"Whoever welcomes a prophet in the name of a prophet will receive a prophet's reward."

MATTHEW 10:41

The Good News always draws us to form community, but being part of a community also stretches us in the direction of the Good News.

We have all been part of communities often enough to be aware how they pull us away from our own self-centeredness into the shared existence of the common life. What we may not be sufficiently aware of is that this stretching is a very necessary part of the Christian life.

It is the community, not the individual, that

believes in the gospel. An individual cannot carry the cross effectively; it is a community effort and responsibility. Only the Christian community as a whole can witness completely to the gospel lifestyle.

In Saint Paul's letter to the Ephesians, he lists a series of "gifts"—which are really functions—that are necessary for a community to sustain itself and continue to grow: "The gifts he gave were that some would be apostles, some prophets, some evangelists, some pastors and teachers, to equip the saints for the work of ministry, for building up the body of Christ" (Ephesians 4:11-12). These functions are the basis for Christian community, and no function is more critical—or more misunderstood—than that of the prophet.

The prophet is one who loves the community and is therefore able to point out deviations from what the community wants itself to be. This function is beyond the scope of merely human reasoning. In other words, a prophet is inspired by God to understand and articulate his or her own experience in a way that challenges the entire community. In this way, the prophet affirms the basic goals of the community and questions the means to those goals.

We need prophets—the more the better—because we are very human and therefore very short-sighted. It's easy for us to get side-tracked in our own personal concerns, prejudices, and ambitions, but prophets will not let us grow complacent.

Although it may seem that today there is more readiness and even openness to letting the prophet speak, let's not mistake the gift of prophecy for an ability to be critical. (A critical mind applied with love is a precious gift, but prophecy depends *solely* on the initiative of God.) Prophets are not usually popular members of a community, and we Christians have not always fared better than other people in listening to our prophets.

The gift of prophecy is not a role gift; it is a function gift. This means that it is not limited to the same one or two members within the community. Anyone at any time may utter a prophetic word—anyone who is open to the Spirit, that is.

Wherever there is a building up of the Body of Christ—which is what Christian community is—there is prophecy. In no way is prophecy limited to homilies or even council meetings, though it can certainly occur in these. Prophecy can take place in a quiet word, a look of understanding and encouragement, or in an encounter that challenges the entire community to put love above anything else. Sometimes the prophetic word can even be spoken in absolute silence, calling the rest of us forth to increasingly deeper silence and prayer.

Wherever one of us asks the questions that make the rest of us face our commitments and our practical living of those commitments, prophecy is present. The word of prophecy transcends the label "liberal" or "conservative," for prophecy is always from the Holy Spirit and reflects the gospel values of truth, love, forgiveness of one another, and childlike dependence on God.

The voice of the prophet is the voice of God among us. So let's listen well for that voice. Let's not be afraid to be challenged by the prophets among us. Let's listen to them, even if we don't like their words straight away.

Spirit of Jesus, give me the ability to respond to the prophetic word when it is spoken to me, and your own courage when I am called to speak it myself.

18

JESUS, LOOK AT ME

Jesus, looking at him, loved him and said, "You lack one thing; go sell what you own, and give the money to the poor, and you will have treasure in heaven; then come follow me."

MARK 10:21

To be looked upon by Christ in the total reality of who we are right now—not after we get some little difficulty worked out, not after we stop acting foolishly or childishly or self-willed—is a moment to be longed for and prayed for. But the eyes of Christ are *always* upon us, and he looks on us with love at all times. It is our task to be aware, to recognize, to believe in the look of the Lord.

Then, after the look, there is the call: "Go, sell what you own, and give the money to the poor...then come follow me." Perhaps our hearts burn when we hear these words, just as the young man's did. Like him, we hear the call, but we doubt we can ever give up "everything." There are still quite a few things we remain attached to, and we wonder if we can ever give them up.

But we miss the point of the call of Jesus to discipleship if we focus on "things." It is not so much our possessions that we must renounce. These material things fall into their appropriate place of importance when we listen to the *whole* call of the Lord: "Come follow me." This is a call to focus our entire attention, hope, and life on Christ. It means that from day to day we let God lead us in everything we do. When we do this, giving up possessions may be the least of our problems.

The call to discipleship isn't a one-time, once-and-for-all event—not for the first disciples and not for us. It's a call that goes on forever and that we must respond to frequently.

The question we need to ask many times a day is: What do you want, Lord, in this situation? I think we'll be surprised at how quickly we "hear" the answer when we get used to asking the question. Of course, we have to want to be led in order to "hear" the answer. It is for us to

be aware, to recognize, to believe that the call of
the Lord is taking place *now*, calling us to follow
him *now*.

Jesus' mother, Mary, is the perfect example
of one who recognized the call of God and responded to his loving gaze with the total gift of
herself at every moment: "Here am I, the servant
of the Lord; let it be with me according to your
word" (Luke 1:39). This is radical discipleship.
Mary heard the call, believed the call, and acted
on the call throughout her life.

Faith is the virtue that allows us to see the
eyes of Christ looking on us in love and empowers us to hear the call of Christ many times
throughout the day. At least once a day in prayer,
simply turn, allow Christ to look on you with
love, and ask: What do you want of me in this
situation? This is faith in practice. Practice it over
and over.

---

*Jesus, you look at me, you call me. Let
me, for once, let go of everything and
ask what you would have me do.*

19

HOSPITALITY

*Let mutual love continue. Do not ne-
glect to show hospitality to strangers, for
by doing that some have entertained
angels without knowing it.*

Hebrews 13:1-2

Recently, I came upon a book of short stories written in "basic French," so I picked it up and felt very proud of myself. After months of studying the language, I can actually read a story all by myself.

One of the stories I read is entitled "The Fourth Poor Man." Here is one of the lines that stuck with me: "My children, welcome the poor, and do not be afraid if there are many; it is not for us to choose. The first may, perhaps, be evil,

87

and even the second and third; it is often the fourth poor man who is good." [4]

While I was still reading that story I received an S.O.S. from a good friend. This mother of two grown children is dealing with her mid-life transition by becoming a freelance writer. She prepares brochures or newsletters for organizations, and her latest client is an ecumenical group that is trying to help refugees on the east coast. She needed just the right Scripture quote to interest people in opening their hearts and homes to refugees, and—since I had encouraged her in this work—she said I owed it to her to deliver the perfect one!

So I delved into the Bible trying to find appropriate references for her project. I didn't find a great many, but the ones I did find, as I told my friend, were uncomfortably convincing.

Jesus' description of the Last Judgment was the first passage that came to my mind: "I was a stranger and you welcomed me" (Matthew 25:35). But the one that struck me most was from the Letter to the Hebrews: "Let mutual love continue. Do not neglect to show hospitality to strangers, for by doing that some have entertained angels without knowing it" (Hebrews 13:1-2).

In the story from the Book of Genesis, Abraham welcomes three strangers who turn out to be three angels of the Lord. When we read this story from the Hebrew Scriptures we can't help but be touched by the delicacy of eastern hospitality. It was the hot part of the day, but Abraham literally *ran* from the cool shade of his tent to greet the travelers, and he *begged* them to rest under his tree and allow him to serve them.

Hospitality is a sacred duty and a trust. Whether it be a stranger—a person whose origin and life is totally unknown to us—or someone who is a well-known friend, it is God whom we receive.

Martha received Christ into her home and served him. Mary received Christ into her home and listened to him. At the monastery, Christ is in our guests—we receive them, serve them as we can, and listen to them. We have experienced in so many ways what blessings have come to us through our guests.

Probably very few of us have ever experienced what it is like to be away from home—from our familiar surroundings and friends, perhaps even in a foreign country—and totally dependent on the kindness of those who receive us. A stranger is very much at the mercy of others. I think that is why the Scriptures make the stranger or foreigner the object of special concern. In fact, the three groups who are singled out to receive care are the widows, the orphans, and...the strangers.

Remember: it is Christ who comes to us in the stranger—or in the friend—in our guests.

Jesus, you invited us to find you in our guests—both friends and strangers. May they too find you in us that we may each discover the beginnings of the kingdom in this sacred exchange.

20

GOOD SPEECH

Death and life are in the power of the tongue.

Proverbs 18:21

The manner in which we speak can contribute to our interior silence. It can allow our inner climate of peace to become an openness to God and to the person or persons with whom we are speaking.

Speech is a powerful instrument for supporting one another in our growth in Christ. There are many words, perhaps spoken quietly and very unselfconsciously, that by their sincerity and care build up and encourage others. Sometimes these words express appreciation or gratitude, and sometimes they may challenge or even correct, but if they are spoken in love, they are "good" speech.

Of course, the disposition of the one receiving the word needs to be one of receptivity and trust. But where the intentions of speaker and listener are in harmony, then the spoken word can contribute to the peace and interior silence of both. Both can become more available to the Spirit of Christ within them.

A mean or untrue word can never heal or build up—no matter how well disposed the hearer. And even if the truth is spoken in love, it still depends on the openness of the hearer in order to bear fruit. Words that are sarcastic, critical, or judgmental foster only disturbance and noise. The only thing that words like these can build up is a false ego. And that's often why we speak them. We try to make ourselves look good by putting someone else down.

In the Rule of St. Benedict, which we follow in the monastery, there is a strong warning about the misuse of words: "We absolutely condemn in all places any vulgarity, gossip, and talk leading to laughter." Saint Benedict thought that the mouth is a door, a door to the inner sanctum, and that door should be sealed to certain kinds of speech. (On the other hand, in his teaching about the one who answers the door at a monastery, Benedict recommends that he or she remember the insight of Sirach 18:17: "Does not a word surpass a good gift?")

We have all experienced again and again that our inner quiet can be enhanced or destroyed by a word. The fact is that words do not come from nowhere. They don't drop down out of the sky. Words proceed out of our hearts.

So if our words are to reflect Christ's healing words, our whole heart needs to be converted totally to Christ *before* we speak. As Paul says in so many ways, we must put on the mind of Christ, think like Christ, hear like Christ. We must learn Christ, so that what comes out of our mouths bears resemblance to Christ.

If we do that, even Benedict would like to hear what we have to say.

Father, master of the good word, close our hearts and lips to all that is evil and destructive. May we put on the mind and heart of Christ, your Son, before we speak.

21

MADE FOR LOVE

(Love) bears all things, believes all things, hopes all things, endures all things. Love never ends.

1 Corinthians 13:7-8

Saint Bernard is a good rhetorician. He makes us love what he points to as most lovable: "What a great thing is love, provided always that it returns to its origin....Flowing back again into its source, it acquires fresh strength to pour itself forth once again."[5]

The teaching of Bernard, as well as that of all our Cistercian Fathers, is primarily one of *charity*. By charity they meant *love of God*, even what has come to be called "mystical marriage" with the Word, which is the direct object and goal of the spiritual life. But he also meant *love of one's brothers and sisters in Christ* as the expression of our pure love of God.

This is not an esoteric teaching. Bernard was a very practical man. He lived in reality. The images he used to illustrate his thoughts are very easily recognizable—like the monks who dozed during his long talks or the fashionable ladies he mentioned in some of his letters. But he was also a far-sighted visionary who sought to draw his brothers and sisters to desire nothing less than fullness of life and love.

We know how weak our love is at times. We constantly experience within ourselves the pull to selfishness, the struggle to let go of resentment, criticalness, and hate. But as Bernard reminds us, our Christian vocation is *love*. We are called to let this love of God flow through us as a channel to the world. Not only in preaching or apostolic work but also in simply praying before the Lord for all and in loving one another. All Christians and all people are called to this love. It is the first *and* the second commandment. It *is* the gospel message.

Love that is isolated, so to speak, from its origin—God—is not great. It is not even true love. Only that love which is poured into us as pure gift (and let's remember every ounce of love within us is pure gift) and returned to its source in gratitude is great. Gratitude is the way in which we make a fitting return for God's gifts to us.

Bernard spoke eloquently of the union of the Word of God with an individual. How is this union brought about? By charity. There is a marriage of the soul with the Word that produces conformity in will, one with the other.

Bernard labored to show that the inequality between the love of the creature and that of the Creator does not make any difference. Where love is concerned there is no measuring: "For although, being a creature, he or she loves less, because he or she is less; nevertheless if he or she loves with his or her whole self, nothing is wanting where all is given." Again he wrote: "Love is the only one of all the movements, feelings and affections of the soul in which the creature is able to respond to its Creator, to repay like with like."

This is a tremendous thing when you think about it. We can, in a sense, be as good at something as God is! And sometimes it's good for us to recognize this great dignity of ours. We need from time to time to stretch beyond our little selves—or at least be open to be stretched—and realize that God is calling us to an actual union in love. This union is real, and it is for all of us—not just for the so-called saints.

We need to be aware of our potential for this union. We need to be so grateful for it that we let our love pour out to others. This is the way love returns to its source.

Yes, my God, I do love you! I thank you with all my heart for this unspeakable privilege. And because I know it is your desire for me, I ask with all my heart the gift of growing in love for others, until I can be love for every person I meet. Don't let me settle for anything less.

22

TRUE LEADERSHIP

"You know that among the Gentiles those whom they recognize as their leaders lord it over them, and their great ones are tyrants over them. But it is not to be so among you; but whoever wishes to become great among you must be your servant."

MARK 10:42-43

It has been rather interesting for me as the abbess of a small monastery to read books and articles on leadership. What strikes me is that only a few of them mention the many gospel texts that link leadership inextricably with service. "Whoever wishes to become great among you must be your servant" (Mark 10:43), Jesus proclaimed.

After saying these words, Jesus did something that no other leader would ever have the courage to do. He spoke of himself as the epitome of true leadership: "The Son of Man came not to be served but to serve, and to give his life as a ransom for the many" (Mark 10:45).

Other great leaders have given their lives in the exercise of leadership: Abraham Lincoln, Mohandas Gandhi, John F. Kennedy, Martin Luther King, Jr. But there is a difference—which I hardly need to point out. The deaths of these men brought great sadness to their own world and certainly to those who followed them, but the death of the Son of Man did more than that. It was both the verification of his mission and the paradigm that he held out to his followers: "Do as I have done" (John 13:15). None of the other slain leaders ever expected that of their followers.

Jesus' death actually revealed to his followers the radically different way he was leading them. Jesus intended to turn the tables on the concept of leadership among his disciples.

In any given society, corporation, or community, the number of designated offices of leadership is limited. You can have only one president, one vice president, one board of trustees, one abbess, one pastor.

But the Gospels say that anyone who influences another (either consciously or unconsciously) to change or to grow is a true leader. Those of us who convey the gospel values and beliefs openly, both by our words and especially by our actions, are leaders. By this definition parents, teachers, and others who influence us deeply are often the best leaders, not only in our personal lives but also in society at large.

This idea of leadership places a good deal of responsibility on every one of us. In reality, none of us can legitimately renege on assuming a leadership role because, whether we like it or not, we've already got it. By the simple fact of living in a society (or community) with other human beings who themselves are at various levels of value-integration, we are all leaders and followers at the same time.

Thus, in a particular situation it could happen that those who hold legitimate authority are not the actual leaders of the community. Ideally speaking, of course, true leadership in the community would be personified in the officials. But true leadership rests in those whose moral qualities and values are stronger and clearer than those of others and who therefore have the authority to challenge others to grow. These persons may or may not be the elected leaders.

Now we come back to Jesus. The values that he presents by his word and in his life are very clear. He says we are to serve one another as he did, even to the point of death. This is no small criterion for leadership.

So whoever among us would be a leader in the ways of the kingdom of God must be the most like Jesus: the one most ready to serve others. That one is the greatest among us--and that one is our true leader.

Each one of us is called to be that one!

Jesus our leader, mold us to the pattern of your way. Make us leaders and followers in loving service. May others grow to their own truth through the example of our lives.

23

THE HOLINESS AROUND US

I beg you to lead a life worthy of the calling to which you have been called, with all humility and gentleness, with patience, bearing with one another in love, making every effort to maintain the unity of the Spirit in the bond of peace. There is one body and one Spirit, just as you were called to the one hope of your calling, one Lord, one faith, one baptism, one God and Father of all, who is above all and through all and in all.

EPHESIANS 4:1-6

In J.D. Salinger's novel *Franny and Zooey,* Franny learns the Jesus Prayer, but in pursuing it without a spiritual guide she gets herself into a state of total mental and psychological exhaustion. She is on the verge of a breakdown.

Her older brother, Zooey, tries to talk with her, but only makes matters worse until he finally hits on the image of Bessie's chicken broth. Franny's mother, Bessie, has been trying to feed her daughter chicken broth, just as she has all her life whenever one of her kids was sick. Franny rejects the broth, but finally Zooey shows her that she has let preoccupation with the words of the Jesus Prayer blind her to the reality of her mother's real gift:

> I'll tell you one thing, Franny. One thing I *know*. And don't get upset. It isn't anything bad. But if it's the religious life you want, you ought to know right now that you're missing out on every single goddam religious action that's going on around this house. You don't even have sense enough to *drink* when somebody brings you a cup of consecrated chicken soup–which is the only kind of chicken soup Bessie ever brings to anybody around this madhouse. So just *tell* me, just tell me, buddy. Even if you went out and searched the whole world for a master– some guru, some holy man–to tell you how to say your Jesus Prayer properly, what good would it do you? How in *hell* are you going to recognize a legitimate

holy man when you see one if you don't even know a cup of consecrated chicken soup when it's right in front of your nose? Can you tell me that?[6]

Like Franny, we can miss the sacred in the everyday and in every person we encounter. We can be so caught up—in our work or our personal concerns or even in our prayer—that we don't see the holiness all around us.

The Spirit is not some vague force in space but a reality in our very lives. Every person is a dwelling place of the Holy Spirit. Saint Paul asks, simply and directly, "Do you not know that you are God's temple and that God's Spirit dwells in you?" (1 Corinthians 3:16).

Just as we would be horrified and broken-hearted to witness the desecration of our chapel or parish church, we should be equally concerned about the sacred temples of our sisters or brothers. We need to be reminded of the sacredness of every person because it is so easy to forget. By way of renewing and encouraging ourselves, therefore, we need to ask ourselves some questions.

Do we truly *reverence* each person with whom we live? This does not mean that we see no weaknesses or areas which need growth in others, but it does mean that we truly reverence everyone as a sacred temple of Christ's spirit. Do we seek to *build up* and not to tear down the other people—each a living temple, remember—with whom we live? Or do we speak critically of others—spreading our own annoyance or anger at particular individuals and so infecting others with the same feelings?

Believe me, anger, resentment, and derision are infectious—just as peace, love, and joy are infectious. Thus, we are all carriers of infection into the Christian community—the question is which kind we predominantly spread.

Only in the context of a very trusted friendship (or perhaps with a spiritual director)—where we are sure that our expressed anger or annoyance at a third party will not cause the recipient of our confidence to think less of the person involved—then and only then are we truly free to share our negative feelings about someone. We do have to work out problems and misunderstandings with others, yes, but not at the cost of another's reputation or esteem in the community. Someone said to me recently, "I don't appreciate hearing another's discontent with someone. I may have my own problem with that person, and I don't need to have it reinforced."

Think about it, and think about Bessie's chicken broth. Let's not miss the goodness of the ever-present Lord in others because of some

quirk that makes someone irritating or even ob-
noxious. The Spirit of Jesus is living in Sam and
Judy and Bill; the Spirit of Jesus is living in Suzie
and Frank and Max; the Spirit of Jesus is living
in Mom and Dad and Sis; and right on through
the community like a litany.

Instead, let's feast one another with the sacred bread of kindness. When Jesus fed the
multitude, it was with ordinary bread–barley
loaves. Yet it prefigured and symbolized the Eucharist. For us the bread we break for one another doesn't prefigure but rather is a continua-
tion of the Eucharist.

---

*Jesus, you knew what it was to be the
target of hostile criticism. The angry
slander about you reached the point of
conspiracy and betrayal, and on the
cross you experienced the ultimate in
indignity and lack of reverence. I am
one of those who mistreat you because
at times I behave with hostility toward
others. I am more anxious to protect
and promote myself than to love. Open
my eyes to the dignity and humanity of
all those whom I'm tempted to desecrate
out of anger or fear or even mere irrita-
tion. My heart's desire is to love you in
every single human being.*

24

A SOURCE OF UNITY

Be aware there is one bread, we who are many are one body, for we all partake of the one bread.

1 Corinthians 10:17

When a group wants to hear one another better, it often forms a circle. When we want to pray in an intimate group, we often join hands and turn and face one another. In a circle, everyone is visible to everyone else. Thus, a circle is a classic symbol of unity.

This is a small point, but when I look at the round host of the Eucharist I am reminded of the oneness of Christ and of each of us in Christ. The Eucharist is a source of Christian unity—one bread of which we all receive a part. This symbolism is visibly more obvious when one loaf is broken into many pieces.

But there is a much deeper reason why the Eucharist is a source of our unity. The Eucharist is both meal and sacrifice. We can't lose sight of its historical context. Jesus, on the night he entered definitively into his own Passover, celebrated the Eucharistic liturgy for the first time. And when his disciples, after his death and resurrection, sought to ritualize this moment, it was with the words, "This is my body that is for you. Do this in remembrance of me" (1 Corinthians 11:24).

The "this" that we are doing "in remembrance" of Jesus is both *meal* and *sacrifice*: We cannot separate the two. It is only because of the sacrifice of Jesus that the Agape—the sharing in love of a meal among us—has significance. If it were not for his sacrifice, this meal would have been the same as every other meal.

It is in this same context of meal and sacrifice that the Eucharist is the source of Christian unity–both in the cloister and in the larger Church. On a natural level, we know that food is directly assimilated into our bodies and becomes the source of our energy–and ultimately of our life. Withdraw all food, and eventually we will cease to live. This is obvious and we experience it palpably. We can touch it. We feel it. The nourishment of the bread of the Eucharist is spiritual, certainly, yet we are equally sure of its life-giving power.

The sacrificial aspect of the Eucharist comes at the very point of its origin: the Eucharist is Christ's body given *for us*. The bread we eat in the Eucharist is broken, and only because it is broken can we eat it. If our most intimate contact with the Risen Lord is in this broken, crucified state, that alone must teach us something about our own lives.

When we study the catechism, we learn that one of the effects of reception of the Eucharist is "transformation into Christ." This sounds so simple and automatic, but we know it is neither. When we eat regular food, we must digest it and transform it into our own substance or we will die. Likewise, the power of the Eucharist is always there, but it is up to us to assimilate it, and when we do we become one with Jesus—and with each other.

I believe this process of assimilation—what actually leads to transformation of all of us into Christ—is the process of conversion...both personal and corporate. We have to be willing to change if the Body of Christ is to become our own flesh and blood. We must choose to let Christ and his values reign in us, contrary to our own selfish desires.

In our personal conversions, we leave our inmost beings open to whatever Jesus asks of us–not only through his direct inspiration but also through the needs and even the desires of others. If we are not changed, if we do not become more ready to respond in love to another, if we are not obedient to one another, if we are not willing to sacrifice ourselves for others, then we have not truly received the Crucified One.

In our corporate conversion, if each of us is becoming more like the bread we share, which is Jesus, then we are also becoming more like each other. In this is our ultimate unity–all of us, together, transformed into the Body of Christ. In so doing, we become bread for each other and bread for the world.

Encircle us with your love, Lord, and make us one, that we may truly become what we eat: your Body, broken and given for others.

25

ENCOURAGEMENT

Blessed be the God and Father of our Lord Jesus Christ, the merciful Father and the God who gives every possible encouragement; he supports us in every hardship, so that we are able to come to the support of others, in every hardship of theirs because of the encouragement that we ourselves receive from God. For just as the sufferings of Christ overflow into our lives; so too does the encouragement we receive through Christ.

2 Corinthians 1:3-5 NJB

The best gift we can give (or receive) from one another is the gift of encouragement. According to Saint Paul, however, *God* is the source of all encouragement. The answer to this seeming contradiction is in the nature of encouragement itself: God encourages and supports each one of us so that we may in turn encourage and support each other.

Paul expresses the entire Paschal Mystery in the simplest of terms: just as the sufferings of Christ overflow into our lives, so too does God's encouragement overflow into our lives.

Encouragement—*paraklesis*—means "consoling help." This help comes first and foremost through God's present and future salvation. The greatest encouragement we can receive is not "You are doing a good job" nor "You are a wonderful person." The greatest encouragement is the conviction that everything in life is leading us further into the kingdom of God that Jesus promised.

Whether we feel fervent or lazy, focused or scattered, our feelings are not the criteria to judge our spiritual state. Encouragement rests, rather, on the mercy of God and on the promises of God. We have to keep coming back to this: Real encouragement comes from God and focuses on the grace of Jesus working in our humdrum lives.

Are we experiencing the death agony of letting go of an attachment? This is Christ's encouragement in us.

Are we struggling to accept ourselves–freckles and failures and all? This is Christ's encouragement in us.

Are we recognizing our half-heartedness regarding prayer ("I'll pray when I have time, but I never seem to have time")? This is Christ's encouragement in us.

Are we simply trying to be faithful each day, working hard and praying as best we can, accepting others even when we feel annoyed? This is Christ's encouragement in us.

Paul continues his theology of encouragement thus: "So if we have hardships to undergo, this will contribute to your encouragement and your salvation; if we receive encouragement, this is to gain for you the encouragement which enables you to bear with perseverance your present sufferings as we do. So our hope for you is secure in the knowledge that you share the encouragement we receive, no less than the sufferings we bear" (2 Corinthians 1:6-7 NJB).

The Spirit of God is the Encourager who helps us recognize the grace of the present moment and let go of anxiety. The Spirit is the Comforter who in times of tension or frustration restores peace in our hearts.

I'm told that the sequoia is a gigantic tree that has very shallow roots. How do they remain

standing during terrible storms? They intercon-
nect their roots and their branches so that when
the fierce winds come they interlock and support each other. That's why they don't fall. So
we pray that the Paraclete, the Comforter, the
Encourager, will continue to come among us to
allow our roots to interlock and support one another.

---

*Jesus, let your paschal encouragement
overflow and fill our lives and the lives
of others. May we always pass on the
graces you give us so that we may be
mutually supported in every storm.*

26

PRAYER AND ACTION

The apostles gathered around Jesus and told him all they had done and taught. He said to them, "Come away to a deserted place all by yourselves and rest a while." For many were coming and going, and they had no leisure even to eat. And they went away in the boat to a deserted place by themselves. Now many saw them going and recognized them, and they hurried there on foot from all the towns and arrived ahead of them. As he went ashore, he saw a great crowd; and he had compassion for them, because they were like sheep without a shepherd; and he began to teach them many things.

MARK 6:30-34

The story of the feeding of the multitude in the Gospel of Mark offers a rather remarkable lesson in prayer and action.

First, Jesus invites the disciples to come away with him to a desert place and be refreshed. In other words, they were to leave all the good work they had been doing to spread the message of the kingdom of God and simply be with the master for a while. Those of us who are contemplatives can certainly relate to that!

Implied in this story, however, is the inevitable tension that arises in the Christian community between activity and service, work and rest, action and contemplation. But perhaps it would be better to call this tension a rhythm rather than polar opposites.

For all Christians there is activity and apostolic service, and then there is the slowing down or changing of activity in order to recuperate and recharge. This interpretation in terms of the rhythm of activity and rest is obvious to those of us who live close to the land, where the changing seasons offer a model for alternating activity. But there is another way of looking at it: There is a rhythm in our relationship with God also.

The call to come away with Jesus into the desert—the place of prayer—is always there. But sometimes the desert-prayer is refreshing and very restful, and at other times the desert is dry, uninviting, and very boring. Though it is always Jesus inviting us, he often seems to go off and leave us alone.

The desert is a place of testing as well as a place of rest. It's true that carelessness and neglect will for sure make prayer more difficult; still, where there is normal fidelity and humility, it is the Lord who decides the time for winter chill and discomfort or summer warmth and fruitfulness. It's for us to remain open and free to respond to what the desert has to offer in any given season of grace.

Prayer is a means to an end. It is a relationship in love that leads us toward union with God. Prayer is utterly necessary for all Christians if we are to transcend ourselves. How better to transcend ourselves than by persevering contact with the Divine Transcendent? This is perfect and complete freedom, the path to perfect love. But to transcend we must be still. We must leave everything behind—all projects and desires, even holy desires—and simply *be toward God*.

Let's remember, however, that our prayer life is not for its own sake. It is for the sake of love. If and when love calls us out of prayer, we must respond. To refuse to leave our prayer for the sake of love is to make prayer an idol.

The story in the Gospel of Mark of the feeding of the multitude points this out. Even though Jesus promised his disciples a desert-prayer experience, the crowds—hungry and needing to be fed—were waiting when they arrived. According to Mark, "He had compassion on them, because they were like sheep without a shepherd." The point of the story, I think, is that sometimes prayer has to wait while love acts.

We know that our revered Saint Benedict dwelt within himself in harmony, always in the presence of his Creator, not allowing his eyes to gaze on distractions. Benedict was a man of prayer, one who could perceive all of creation within one ray of divine light. Isn't this what each of us desires? Yet we also know that Benedict spent his entire life in the service of others. To dwell within ourselves in harmony, then, we often have to go out of ourselves in love.

Let's recommit ourselves to a life of prayer, remembering that prayer is only for the sake of love. Like the disciples, we must be ready with Jesus to abandon even the enjoyment of prayerful rest when the needs of others ask this of us. No matter where we are or who we are, we all have to practice our commitment to prayer while being equally sensitive and open to the call of the multitude.

Father, let the gift of prayer continue to grow in us. Keep us watchful in prayer to the needs of others, ready to act in love as your Son taught us and true to his teaching until your glory is revealed in us.

Fall

27

FIDELITY WILL COST ALL

*Ruth said, "Do not press me to leave you
or to turn back from following you!
Where you go, I will go: Where you
lodge, I will lodge; your people shall be
my people, and your God my God."*

RUTH 1:16

The beginning of September is a rather important time for most people, though for different reasons and with quite different feeling tones. For young people, it's "back to school." For adults, it's Labor Day Weekend—a holiday that sort of softens the blow that summer vacations are over and it's back to work. For Trappistines at our Abbey in Iowa, September marks the beginning of what we have come to call our "Candy

Season," a time of concentrated work in our little candy factory. But September first is also a very important day for another reason: It is the day on which we honor Ruth, one of the very great women of the Old Testament.

When I think of the biblical Ruth, two aspects of her life loom very large for me. First, Ruth was an alien, a displaced person, a foreigner in a strange land. Second, Ruth was faithful—to her family, her people, her values, and her calling. In our world today, there are many displaced persons and precious little fidelity.

I don't know if there are more people living in lands other than their own today than ever before. Maybe it's one of those social problems that always seem worse in one's own time but actually has always existed. But the fact is, we know that many people around the globe have been forced to leave their country for one reason or another.

I wonder if most of us can even begin to imagine what it is like to be uprooted from one's very culture, not to mention from family and friends and familiar and dear places. And then there is the difficulty of learning a new language when you long to hear only your own native language, to understand everything being said and not just a word here or there. Being a stranger in a strange land always involves insecurity, perhaps physical danger, and certainly the work of adapting to a whole new way of life.

Ruth, a young widow, accepted the need to leave her own land and people. Her mother-in-law, Naomi, needed her, and so she went. For Ruth, the story ends happily with a picture of herself and her new husband Boaz holding hands and looking on proudly as Naomi bounces baby Obed on her knees.

It doesn't always end so neatly. One who chooses to be faithful and accepts the consequences may suffer a lot and for a long time.

What does the story of Ruth tell us? Her fidelity underlines for us the important truth that our life choices are personal and commit us to others. In marriage, for example, one spouse does not promise to love and cherish the institution of marriage but rather the real, flesh-and-blood person of the other spouse—not just as he or she is now but also as he or she will be in 20, 30, 50, even 60 years! In religious life, we make a commitment to the individuals in our community, not to the institution itself.

In our very fidelity to spouse or community we may be called to let go of our security, of what is most familiar and dear to us. We may be called to change our ideas, our habits, even perhaps our homeland. Fidelity will cost all.

Because of the total commitment it demands, fidelity happens only when we consistently maintain contact with the beloved. Someone in the family of a recently divorced couple said to me: "They were apart too much." Something snapped in the bond; a marriage can't endure too much physical distance. The same can happen in the cloister. We've got to be in relationship with each other and with God at all times.

Ruth is the model for fidelity. She was faithful to the ones she loved, even at the cost of leaving all that she had grown accustomed to. Are we willing to become "aliens" to our own cherished ways or ideas in order to be faithful?

Jesus, forever faithful in our alien world, strengthen us in our commitment to our commitments and relationships.

28

THE MANNER IS ORDINARY

*There (Joseph) made his home in a town
called Narareth.*

MATTHEW 2:23

Saint Joseph encompasses the paradox of the extraordinary in the ordinary, the glory in the common, the saintly in the everyday.

Joseph is the patron saint of all workers, whom we honor every Labor Day. He was a craftsman, a carpenter to be exact. In an agricultural and pastoral civilization such as his, the village carpenter was something like the local handyman today. When a yoke broke or a plow handle was bent, the farmers would go to Joseph for replacement parts. And while the carpenter was indispensable in Nazareth, his place

127

in society was not considered very prestigious. (We know this from the rather derogatory tone of the townspeople when they questioned the parentage of the wonder worker, Jesus of Nazareth: Isn't he the *carpenter's* son? In other words, he was no big deal.)

I imagine Joseph was a sensitive man. He listened to dreams—way before Freud and Jung—and acted on them. But he did so in a way that was quiet and matter-of-fact. He had the gift of making momentous decisions based on his intuition and spiritual sensitivity. His attitude was low-key, his style unspectacular.

We can draw an important lesson from Joseph. It is in the steady rhythm of going to work, raising a family, living in community, growing older that we find God. If we could see our own lives—the actual flow from moment to moment—with x-ray vision, we might recognize that hidden in the most common activity is the seed of God's glory.

As we look at Joseph's life with hindsight, we see that beneath its ordinary appearance the most earth-shattering event of all time took place: God became a human being, literally under his roof. The words of Jesus, "The kingdom of God is among you" (Luke 17:21), were most true in his own family. The glory of God was hidden there, like a precious jewel within an ordinary clay vessel.

Meister Eckhart once wrote that it is delusion to think that we can obtain more of God by contemplation or pious devotions than by being at the kitchen hearth or working in the merchants' stalls. This is hard to believe because it is literally beyond human comprehension. God is in the saucepan as well as the chalice, the lawn mower as well as the monstrance. The manner is ordinary, but God's glory is in every event, every moment, every particle of creation.

To some of us, this may sound a bit intimidating. It sounds as if we may be saying, "We'd better watch out, God is at our elbow, ready to catch us in our mistakes." But there is another way of understanding it: Yes, God is at our elbow, because there is no part of creation in which God is not present, but we need only to live in harmony with that divine presence.

Joseph, the carpenter, the husband, and the father, will help us.

Lord Jesus, like Joseph let us see your glory in the ordinary things of life. May we always be mindful that God is at our elbow.

29

CIRCLES OF SOLITUDE

*Always be ready to make your defense
to anyone who demands from you an
accounting for the hope that is in you,
yet do it with gentleness and reverence.*

1 PETER 3:15-16

"You must honor everyone" is the eighth Instrument of Good Works in the Rule of St. Benedict, followed immediately by "...and never do to another what you do not want done to yourself."

A line from the German poet, Rainer Maria Rilke, is a great commentary on those words. He says that love "consists in this, that two solitudes protect and border and salute each other." [7]

Thus, to love others requires that we first reverence, honor, and salute them in their solitude. This is a very respectful stance for us to take. It does not invade others either by curiosity or by force or by manipulation.

God is the source and model of such reverent love. Who leaves us more free, who respects our solitude more than God?

Saint Benedict says that we are to render this reverence to all. This is the core of the challenge of love. We don't need to agree with others; we need to reverence them. We don't need to be their confidant or to influence others; we need to honor their mystery and uniqueness as persons.

This sense of reverence does not always flourish in communities or even families. We tend to think that because we live daily with people we know all there is to know about them. No matter how well we know people, however, there are always surprises, hidden strengths, and gifts. Besides, people do change, although often we don't notice because we're not honoring their borders.

Rilke's point is that love exists when *two* solitudes "protect and border and salute each other." Notice, it is not just a matter of respecting the solitude of the other; we must also develop our *own* solitude before we can border that of another. There is a deep truth here. To truly love, we must have a center from which to reverence and honor others.

In other words, we have to be at home with ourselves, accepting our own flaws and wonderful qualities. This kind of self-acceptance comes ultimately in prayer, where we meet the source of our being and say yes—both to our creator and to ourselves.

To honor others reverently, we must refrain from using them to fulfill our needs, from projecting onto them our own pain. I have this mental picture of community (really, any society) as endless circles of solitude. The circles sometimes bump into each other; sometimes avoid each other, sometimes invade each other. If solitudes "border" one another, however, they honor the boundaries that are necessary for each individual to live and grow.

Just a word about boundaries. In a Christian community, we can cross one another's boundaries very easily. It can be in little or more significant ways, physically or just in our minds. Love protects the solitude of others, and this has nothing to do with being extroverted or introverted. We can cross boundaries and invade the solitude of another out of simple curiosity, but none of us has a right to know the personal matters of others unless they want to share them. If they choose not to, we must honor that choice.

Circles of solitude not only border; they protect. But to "border," in Rilke's sense, I think, also means to be there for others, to care and notice signals of distress—while always respecting their freedom and uniqueness.

In practical terms, there are two main points about circles of solitude. First, we must construct our own circle, letting solitude lead us down into our own depths, where God, who is our center, can reveal our true selves. Second, we must learn to border our circles with those of others, developing a deep sense of reverence for every other person, no matter what his or her personality or character traits or flaws.

Lord, help us to honor every person with a halo of reverence. May we seek you at our deepest center and learn to border the circles of solitude of all others.

30

DISCIPLINED DISCIPLES

*Now that is not the way you learned
Christ! For surely you have heard about
him and were taught in him, as truth
is in Jesus. You were to put away your
former way of life, your old self.*

EPHESIANS 4:20-22

"Discipline" is one of those words that is sweet
and sour. It attracts and repels at the same time.
On the one hand, it is a strong word. It connotes
order, and we all know that we need a certain
amount of order to live in peace and freedom.
No one knows better than those of us in a monastery that unchecked license does not breed
happiness!

But on the other hand, parts of us find the

very thought of discipline distasteful, something to be avoided. Again, we in monastic life have seen the excesses and misuses of discipline enough to know that it has a "dark side." Part of the reason for this contradictory reaction is that the term "discipline" has several meanings. It can refer to a code of conduct or a set of spiritual practices, or it can mean punishment or even self-inflicted mortification.

So let's define discipline as "a quality of orderliness gained through self-control." Under this definition, anything that is worth doing or learning requires a certain discipline. To play a musical instrument, for example, one has to practice. And it isn't sufficient to practice one hour today but only five minutes the next week and ten minutes three weeks later. Forget it. There has to be discipline in the time, the setting, even in the way we practice. In this sense, then, discipline frees us to do what we want to do. It provides the optimum conditions for learning and growing.

When we are children, discipline is imposed from the outside, mostly by our parents and teachers. We must do our homework and go to bed at a certain time. We must practice the piano every day or mow the lawn once a week.

Part of growing up, however, is to develop the ability and the will to discipline ourselves, by our own choice and for our own good and the good of others. Adults choose discipline not for its intrinsic worth but for what it leads to: We want to keep our job, we arrive to work on time; we want to lower our golf score, we play at least once a week; we want to lose weight, we jog every morning.

In a similar way, we adult Christians choose to discipline our spiritual lives. We do so not for its intrinsic worth but for what it leads to: prayer (or union with God) and charity (love and service of our sisters and brothers). Prayer and charity don't happen automatically. They happen when we choose to build them into the structure of our lives. Remember the Little Prince and his fox in the book by Antoine de Saint-Exupéry? The Little Prince learned that the task of winning the trust and friendship of the fox could be accomplished only by coming to meet him at the same time each day.

The word "discipline" is related to the word "disciple." In Latin *discere* means "to learn, to know"; *discipline* means "learning." All of us, through Baptism, become disciples of Christ, which means that we must take our life in Christ seriously and learn what it really means—and that takes discipline. If we remember that discipline is an adult decision that leads to discipleship, we might find it attractive and worthy of our effort.

*Make us disciplined disciples, O Christ.
Give us the discipline of freedom and
the freedom of discipline.*

31

JESUS LEADS US

And (Jesus) said to them, "Go into all the world and proclaim the good news to the whole creation."

MARK 16:15

A person cannot be a leader in isolation; that would be a contradiction in terms. One is a leader only in relation to a community. This is important. A religious community *makes* a leader—and not just by legally electing someone or accepting someone who is assigned a leadership role. It goes much deeper than that. A community *enables* someone—usually one of their ranks—to be leader. (It is interesting that the word "enabling" now has a negative connotation, as in "enabling" someone's chemical dependency.

But in a positive sense, many people—such as doctors, teachers, or spiritual directors—enable people to become more responsible for their own life.)

An abbess once shared with me her experience after her election. She was so shocked that she asked for a recount to make sure that a mistake hadn't been made. She told them, "I need you to enable me to be your abbess."

Leaders *need* the community to enable them—not by compliments or flattery but by a sincere faith response. And this response is not a once and for all thing; it's a constantly renewed attitude and gesture. A leader can be the wisest, holiest, most learned person in the world, but if the community does not enable him or her to be Christ among them, the leader's efforts will be thwarted.

A person in Church leadership is to convey by word and deed the teaching of Christ and his unconditional and universal love. Obviously one who is called *by virtue of his or her office* to seek God's will in all things *must* put aside personal preferences and prejudices and be totally at the service of Christ. Far from being able to indulge his or her own fancies, the leader is to be truly selfless in seeking Christ in and for the community.

The leader must be earnest in discovering God's will, and this demands the outlay of a considerable amount of energy. The leader is called to perceive, to be mindful, to foresee, to practice discretion, to reflect, to listen to everyone, to process information, to make decisions, and then to act in the name of Christ.

The leader is a central figure. He or she is not above the community but more like the hub of a wheel: one who is a point of unity, equally close or accessible to all, a source of strength (and challenge) to each member. But more than anything, a leader must be one who embodies Christ's presence.

There is danger in overstating the role of leader in order to pinpoint the responsibilities of leadership. It is not true that the community is totally dependent on its leaders and will be only as good as they are. In fact, a community is only as good as each individual person within it. The community will be as motivated, as charitable and tolerant, as forgiving and kind, as prayerful and holy as each individual member.

But having said that, I would like to talk about one of the most important functions of leadership, that of teaching. Everything a Christian leader teaches should—like the leaven of divine justice—permeate the minds of his or her followers. The principal teaching is the word of

God. The function of mediating the word of God is foremost in the function of the leader of any religious community. He or she is not necessarily more learned or clever than anyone else, but the leader does need to be in touch with the gospel and able to discern the word of God in the hearts of others. The leader must then be able to articulate that word for the community.

This ministry of the word, this constant reiteration of truths that everyone already knows and assents to, is a very important means of maintaining a cohesiveness within the Christian community. There are many and varied ways for this teaching to be channeled through the community. We know that the leader's own life and conduct is going to speak as loudly—if not more loudly—than anything he or she says. Like it or not, leaders do teach by their attitudes, choices, manner of dealing with persons and situations—because all of these reveal the values that they really live by. (I do make a plea that we bear in mind a leader's human weakness and limitations and every person's—including a leader's—need for growth.)

What are the corresponding responsibilities of the other members of a community? Willingness to listen and learn and change? Certainly. Openness and candor about themselves? Of course. Desire to grow and to be challenged? Without a doubt. Yes to all of these and more.

But in addition I think every person in a community shares the responsibility to teach. Each one is called to preach and to mediate the word—not necessarily in formal talks, although this will be part of it for many, but in the same primary way that leaders do: by living the gospel.

So let all of us—leaders and members alike—accept our responsibility to allow Jesus to speak and act through us. It is Jesus who ultimately leads us, and all of us are his followers.

Jesus, bless each member of our community—leaders and members alike—that we may cry the gospel with our lives, by our attitudes and choices, by our acceptance of our own weaknesses and failures.

32

GOD'S WORK

Moses said to Joshua, "Choose some men for us and go out, fight with Amalek. Tomorrow I will stand on the top of the hill with the staff of God in my hand." So Joshua did as Moses told him, and fought with Amalek, while Moses, Aaron, and Hur went up to the top of the hill. Whenever Moses held up his hand, Israel prevailed; and whenever he lowered his hand, Amalek prevailed. But Moses' hands grew weary; so they took a stone and put it under him, and he sat on it. Aaron and Hur held up his hands, one on one side, and the other on the other side; so his hands were steady until the sun set. And Joshua defeated Amalek and his people with the sword.

EXODUS 18:8-13

The story of the Israelites' battle with Amalek is a great tale. Joshua and his warriors are down in the valley fighting Amalek. Moses is up on the hill with the staff of God in his hand. Aaron and Hur are there with Moses, supporting his arms as he raises them in prayer. Then there's this see-saw action: As Moses' arms rise up in prayer, Joshua wins the battle; as Moses lets his arms fall, Amalek wins the battle.

Who is doing the greater work? Joshua battling down there in the heat? Moses doing the praying? Aaron and Hur supporting Moses' arms? I think the whole point of the story is that *God* is doing the work. This is *God's* battle. It is *God's* people who are being brought to the Land of Promise. But God can't do it without Joshua to fight and Moses to intercede and Aaron and Hur to support Moses' arms. This battle is God's work, but God must act through the work of these mortal men.

Each one of us has a little of Joshua in us. He had to struggle with a tendency toward jealousy, impatience, hypersensitivity, and discouragement. Like Joshua, we can sometimes feel overwhelmed with the tasks laid on our shoulders.

But we also have Moses in our nature. We have all experienced his spirit of total faith in God, his conviction that the Promised Land is

just around the corner. But the Moses in us sometimes gets tired and discouraged.

What about Aaron and Hur? Are they part
of our personal spirituality package? Aaron, on
the right, may symbolize the support we receive
from our individual, private prayer. Hur, on the
left, may call to mind our communal prayer with
the entire Church, which goes on even when
we are only half present or half awake.

In a sense everything is God's work, but
God somehow and for some reason needs us to
accomplish it. So struggle we must, and have
faith we must, and pray we must.

---

*Lord God, bring to completion all you
have in mind for us as we strive to do
your work.*

33

INVOLUNTARY SOLITUDE

"Come away to a deserted place all by yourselves and rest a while."

MARK 6:31

Most of us are happy to enter into solitude when the opportunity arrives. Parents, busy workers, community activists feel the need for it almost as much as—or maybe even more than—contemplative monks and nuns.

After his disciples returned from busy missionary activity, Jesus would invite them to "come away to a deserted place." The solitude Jesus chose was usually short-lived. He always responded first to the needs of others, but he kept returning to prayer and solitude in order to revitalize himself and his followers.

The lives of contemporary disciples of Jesus are also filled with activity, most of which is necessary and some of which is not. We, too, need time to be apart, to rest in the Lord, to be absorbed in prayer. Thus we will be refreshed, to return to our daily activity with a deeper inner quiet and calm.

We call this kind of solitude "voluntary," and such solitude is a great blessing. But there is such a thing as involuntary solitude, an apartness from others that we have *not* chosen. In each of our lives there are moments when we are alone and do not wish to be. This happens for some when they become elderly. For others, it happens when they are ill for long periods of time or are mourning the death of a loved one. Still others can feel isolated when they are unemployed or lacking in meaningful work. Some even have a sense of isolation when a misunderstanding occurs or when their ideas are not shared with enthusiasm by others. There is no one who has not experienced this sense of involuntary isolation.

God, however, can use these times for our spiritual growth and development. During these occurrences of involuntary solitude, we can kick and scream and curse our fate, or we can use them as opportunities to retreat to the desert, where God can speak to our hearts. When our solitude has ended, we often can look back and see why God led us into the desert and what it has done for our soul.

One caution must be mentioned, however. When we do experience this kind of involuntary solitude, whatever the cause, it is wise to speak of it with a trusted friend or professional. This is not a form of escape or avoidance—just the opposite. It is an attempt to deal with the reality of what we are experiencing. Escape or evasion comes when we try to fill every waking minute with noise, entertainment, reading, idle talk, and unnecessary activity just to make ourselves feel that we aren't really alone or lonely. Sharing the burden of our involuntary solitude with others does not remove the pain, but it does keep us in touch with reality.

Transformation and inner freedom can grow out of our inner struggle to accept our involuntary isolation. It can throw us on the mercy and love of our God. Just as we all enjoy voluntary, chosen solitude, we also need to remember that we must bear the burden of our own and others' involuntary solitude.

Lord Jesus, lead us into the desert and give us the grace to gratefully embrace all the solitude you offer—both voluntary and involuntary. May it help us grow ever closer to you.

34

WHAT NEEDS TO BE HEALED

*They brought to him a deaf man who
had an impediment in his speech; and
they begged him to lay his hand on him.
He took him aside in private, away from
the crowd, and put his fingers into his
ears, and he spat and touched his
tongue. Then looking up to heaven, he
sighed and said to him, "ephphatha,"
that is, "Be opened," and immediately
his ears were opened, his tongue was
released, and he spoke plainly.*

MARK 7:32-35

There's real intimacy and power in the entire
scene between Jesus and the deaf man who is
also a mute. (Actually the gospel says he had a
"speech impediment." Maybe it was something

as simple as a stammer.) The man can't even speak his own need; his friends must speak it for him. But Jesus meets the man where he is and goes right to the heart of his need. And Jesus doesn't embarrass the man in public but rather takes him aside, out of the way of prying eyes and wagging tongues.

Jesus enters into the new creation process. He heals in the name of the one who sent him, the Father. He gives this man back the powers to hear and to speak, but now they are a sign of the kingdom of God.

If we can enter into this gospel scene in a real way, we will learn something interesting about ourselves *and* about God. Here we are, the crowd of us, walking along a road. There is Jesus coming toward us, surrounded by his friends. A few of you take me by the arm and lead me to Jesus and ask him to heal me. Then we bring Betty over so she will be healed. Then we bring Mary Ann and Ken and Theresa and Tom to be healed...but of what?

What are our sicknesses? What is it about ourselves that needs to be healed? Maybe our companions and friends can articulate it better than we can ourselves.

We do reveal to one another our needs, our points of sickness, our compulsions, our sins.

Thanks be to God! As painful as it is to name them, we need to recognize what needs to be healed in us. For we will never know the depths of the love and mercy of God until we have stood before Jesus—exposed, totally as we are, with no excuses and defenses—and asked for his help.

As wounded as we are, if we are willing to expose ourselves to the look of Jesus, his loving mercy will heal us. And he will not embarrass us. He will take us aside and speak the word that only we need to hear.

We need to let others bring us to Jesus, and we must bring others to Jesus.

Lord, we praise you for the power of that tender mercy that heals all who come to you and ask for what they need.

35

THE GOOD OF OTHERS

Let each of you look not to your own interest, but to the interests of others.

PHILIPPIANS 2:4

We struggle to know how to love, to know what it really means for us in our daily lives. And then—POW—the gospel message hits us between the eyes: We are not just to love and serve the people with whom we have chosen to share our lives. The gospel offers us our "enemies" to love—those who really don't like us, those who would gladly make fun of us or even hurt us if they had the opportunity.

Living out this vision of love doesn't come easily or naturally for us. In Saint Paul's letters, he teaches us this practice: "Do not seek your own advantage, but that of the other" (1 Corinthians 10:24).

Practicing love requires a concrete plan. We need to keep it simple. We can't wait for extraordinary opportunities. Five minutes of love today is worth more than the promise of martyrdom tomorrow. So we move along, doing what we can to really let the teaching of Jesus—and, even more, his example—mold us, form us.

There is no better way to enter into practicing love than with a commitment right now to the good of others—those we love, those who love us, and those whom we do not love or who do not love us.

Jesus, help me to do one good deed today for someone I love, for someone who loves me, for someone I don't love, and for someone who doesn't love me.

36

MOURNFUL JOY

"Blessed are those who mourn, for they will be comforted."

I once walked with a friend who had been diagnosed with cancer. He and his wife had three children—eight, six, and three at the time. I was amazed that even in the midst of the worst part of his illness, he had come to unbelievable peace. He and his wife had not let their grief overcome them. Months later, the news of his complete cure was almost anti-climactic, although he expressed a tremendous sense of gratitude to God.

This experience taught me that from the depths of fear, pain, and agonizing uncertainty can arise an exuberant but very deep joy. I think that this is the point of the beatitude, "Blessed are those who mourn, for they shall be comforted."

Of course it only stands to reason that when a person rises from near death to full life, it will not be taken lightly. But on a deeper level, it seems that our capacity for real joy is inseparable from our capacity for real distress or grief. These realities in our lives are somehow tied to one another.

Kahlil Gibran in *The Prophet* says this in a poetic way: "The self same well from which your laughter rises was oftentimes filled with your tears." [8] In other words, the deeper that sorrow carves space into our being, the more joy we can contain.

To understand this paradox better, it helps to differentiate between sorrow/mourning and sadness/melancholy. There is a difference, although in our use of these words we don't always distinguish between the two emotions— similar on the surface but far from the same, for one robs us of joy; the other prepares us for joy. ("Melancholy" is defined in the dictionary as "depressed, low spirited, dark-colored" and "mourning" means "to grieve over a loss.")

The mourning that is called "blessed" by the Lord may be the loss of a loved one (that is what we usually think of, for example, on All Souls Day) or it may be a more pervasive, general sense of our limitations as human beings, our lack of wholeness, our ultimate mortality.

Saint Augustine links this beatitude, "Blessed are they who mourn," with the gift of the Holy Spirit called "knowledge." What he means is that a true knowledge or understanding of the human condition begets mourning. "Our hearts are restless," says Augustine, simply. What saves this blessed mourning from turning into the evil of melancholy? Only hope: "...until they rest in you, O Lord," Augustine concludes.

Sometimes I wonder if I speak too often of the pain and struggle and darkness and dryness in life and not enough of the very real beauty and loveliness of life. This may be, but one thing I do know: If we go one inch below the surface in ourselves or others, we find disappointment. Some have more, some have less, but it's impossible to find a person who feels totally whole and understood, fully loved and able to love, and completely at peace.

Many of us agree with the person who once said: "God save us from bossy attempts to oblige us to be cheered up." We have to come to terms with our existential, very real grief at the human condition. Then, and only then, can transcendental joy flow.

For Christians, we do this by uniting our pain and darkness with the redeeming pain and darkness of the Lord Jesus. Uniting our suffering with his does not take it away, but it does allow us to bear it with hope. "Our hearts are restless, until they rest in you, O Lord."

The presence of struggle and heartache in our lives does not bar us from true joy. On the contrary, it can prepare our hearts for fuller and deeper joy. The only real enemy of joy is a melancholy that turns us inward on ourselves and makes us lose hope. Blessed, indeed, are we who mourn, *because* we shall be comforted.

Lord, may that little winged thing called hope turn all our mourning into joy, until that day of bliss when all tears are taken away.

37

WE NEED EACH OTHER

Now there was a woman who had been suffering from hemorrhages for twelve years. She had endured much under many physicians, and had spent all that she had; and she was no better, but rather grew worse. She had heard about Jesus, and came up behind him in the crowd and touched his cloak, for she said, "If I but touch his clothes, I will be made well." Immediately her hemorrhage stopped; and she felt in her body that she was healed of her disease.

MARK 5:25-28

I can hardly hear the gospel story of the woman with the hemorrhage without recalling the lyrics of a song one of our Sisters likes to sing: "It takes a lot of courage for a woman to reach out to a stranger in her need." Jesus was once asked, "Who is my neighbor?" and responded with the parable of the Good Samaritan, the one who takes care of a stranger.

There's a twist in the story of the woman, however. The one in need reaches out to the stranger *in a crowd*. One solitude touches another solitude in the midst of hundreds of others. Imagine the dynamic operating here. I don't understand electricity at all, with its positive and negative poles, but this story has the explosive force of two powerful opposites attracting each other like great magnets. What are the two poles? *Need* and *power,* brought together in a crowd by the force of faith.

The need is no little pin prick. This was a debilitating disease that had consumed this woman's life, strength, and resources. Saint Mark is very explicit. She was poor from doctors' bills, yet her condition was worse than ever. She was so low that she had nothing to lose. Perhaps this is what gave her the courage to act. She "had heard," in one way or another, the good news about Jesus, and she believed. (The Gospel of Mark is a feminist's delight. Women are invariably the true disciples, and this story is a case in point. The disciples don't know what's going on and even chide Jesus for his naive question "Who touched me?")

But Jesus knew that real power had been released. In a sense, the power to cure her disease could not be restrained, even by Jesus. It leapt out of him when he was touched by such faith as the woman's. Only later did Jesus say, almost as an afterthought, "Daughter, your faith has made you well. Go in peace, and be healed of your disease" (Mark 5:34).

This powerful and touching vignette is at heart a conversion story. This is more than a miracle to prove Jesus' divinity; it's a moment of conversion leading to discipleship. The woman heard, she believed, she reached out, she was changed. She responded by falling at Jesus' feet in compunction and gratitude. Isn't this what we are all called to do?

Another player in this story is the crowd itself. Each of us touches Jesus within a community, within a crowd, so to speak. Conversion takes place within the community. Perhaps that crowd around the woman was more like a supportive community than a cursory reading would indicate. It was from others (in the crowd?) that she had heard about Jesus. It may well have been the enthusiasm and faith of the crowd that gave her the courage to move towards Jesus. And I don't think it's forcing the facts to imagine the joy of the people around her when they saw the work of God that Jesus had performed. (The Gospels are full of the wonder and joy of people witnessing Jesus' ministry.) So this conversion of a person who had so long been tormented by sickness is within the context of a crowd, a community.

Christians are a walking crowd of histories, jostling each other at times, carrying each other at other times. We need each other. Most likely the word that will lead us to Jesus, the word that will turn our needs towards his power in faith, will come to us from this crowd around us. We need each other, in a sense, to conceal ourselves as we grope toward Jesus. And we need each other as our wounds are finally uncovered, because even in a Christian community we realize that no sickness is so utterly unique that many others don't share it.

It was because of the crowd that the woman had the courage to reach out to a stranger in her need, and it is because of the crowd that we will be able to do the same.

Lord Jesus, grant us the courage to reach out to you in community and be healed.

38

SELF-TRANSCENDENCE

"The king will say to those at his right hand 'Come, you that are blessed by my Father, inherit the kingdom prepared for you from the foundation of the world.'"

MATTHEW 25:34

Death is real and leads to a radically different mode of existence.

Saint Benedict's injunction in his Rule to keep death daily before our eyes is one of his deepest spiritual maxims. It is not morbid or masochistic to *live* in the awareness of our own death. This does not mean thinking about how we will meet death twenty years from now. That kind of concern would be totally useless. (Most of us have painted our own deathbed scene a few times, maybe including in it the odor of sanctity. That's not keeping death before our eyes; that's keeping a *fantasy* of death before our eyes.)

Death is here and now, right before our eyes, however, because in fact the moment of death is unknown. The moment of our death lies in the will of God alone.

Deep prayer, especially silent prayer and what contemplatives call "non-felt" prayer, can be the privileged moment of facing and accepting our death. Perhaps it is for this reason that we resist prayer. Our daily activities, which we often use to avoid keeping death before our eyes, constantly impinge on our prayer time. If we want to know how strongly we resist death, we have an easy checkpoint: How deeply do we resist the silence of prayer?

But it is precisely in the silence of prayer that we are brought to live on the edge of our existence, and it is only there that we can more deeply perceive the splendor and giftedness of life.

One of the titles we give Jesus is "Christ the King." Perhaps we say these words glibly, not knowing what they really mean. None of us ever lived under monarchy. But although Christ's kingship is not of this world, it is intimately related to the life and death of each of us.

First of all, Jesus revealed to us the true nature of God. But he also reveals to us the true nature of our own divine potential. At every moment of our lives, we are drawn from incompleteness to completeness. This is a process that many contemporary theologians are calling "self-transcendence."

Self-transcendence allows us to extend ourselves *out*—to reach out to others to give and to receive from others the gift of fulfillment. And the ultimate point of self-transcendence is our acceptance of death. The acceptance of death is the final *yes* to the realization that *only* God can fill our emptiness. In the silence of prayer we turn totally unarmed and totally receptive to the giver of life and accept whatever our life will be.

Self-transcendence is a moment of gratitude, when we realize, perhaps hazily, that what we had believed we were doing for ourselves—all our intrigues and plans for self-fulfillment and happiness—have really done nothing to fill the void in our true selves. All we have at that moment is the realization that we have received gifts in life that allowed us to move beyond ourselves, and this realization gives us the faith and hope that on the other side of the silence of death there will be total self-transcendence in the next life, whatever that may be like.

Jesus Christ is a true king. The Father has

given him power over all creation, and through his resurrection he has power even over death. Our faith in this power of Jesus is what gives us the courage to face the silent unknown of death *and* the power to live in the silence of prayer.

Lord Jesus, we pray that we may not be afraid to live on the edge of existence, to live radically open to life and to death in self-transcending love.

Winter

39

WATCHING AND WAITING

It is good that one should wait quietly
for the salvation of the Lord.

LAMENTATIONS 3:26

There is something unremitting in the movement of the liturgical seasons. Whether we feel ready or not, we are swept into a powerful current, carried places, perhaps, we would prefer not to go. If we were to begin Advent when we felt ready, who knows when it would begin? We might see in this an example of how in the spiritual life we cannot always go by our subjective systems but must sometimes yield to that which is outside ourselves. This is what enables us to transcend our own limited views and feelings.

And so, at the beginning of winter, we also

begin a new liturgical year and enter into the season of anticipation that we call Advent. Each one of us brings to a particular Advent season ten, twenty, fifty, even seventy Advents past. What can possibly be said that we have not heard and thought about many times before? But that attitude is a mistake, for it shortens the arm of God. We must let the Lord lead us through this season as though we had never been here before—because, in fact, we haven't.

I heard a story about a dying nun in the last stages of cancer, who was awaiting the coming of her Lord with every ounce of physical and spiritual energy she had left. Her nurse relayed that during the Sister's last relapse, when it seemed quite possible that they might lose her, she heard her say several times, "Come, Jesus."

Those two words are the archtypal prayer of Advent. After the Lord's Prayer, it is also the prayer par excellence of the Christian at all times. In those two words is expressed the whole Paschal Mystery: Christ, the Son of God made flesh, anointed in death and raised in resurrection, who reveals the love of the Father, has come and will come again in power and glory in the cosmic transformation of this universe as well as in the humblest death of every person.

What the Church through the liturgy calls us to, however, is not simply to wait four weeks for the celebration of Christmas nor to wait patiently for the second coming of the Lord nor even to wait for Jesus to take us to heaven when we die. Waiting is part—but only part—of the Advent season. As in the parable of the ten virgins at the wedding feast, we must *watch* and wait.

If—as monks often experience during the busy weeks before Christmas—prayer is falling asleep on one's feet, I hope at least that the line from the Song of Songs applies: "I slept, but my heart was awake!" (Song of Songs 5:2). Because wakefulness is what the Lord asks of us: "Beware, keep alert, for you do not know when the time will come" (Mark 13:33). Watchfulness implies a certain sobriety, a renunciation of the excesses associated with the "night." To be watchful is not only to stay awake, but it is to guard our thoughts and desires, to watch over the actions of our life. It is what we have come to understand from the Buddhist tradition as "mindfulness" in the fullest meaning of the term.

Advent is a reminder to us that we Christians are called to be watchers. Each deepening winter night is a symbol of our life-long vigil— our waiting, watching, praying for the Lord to come in glory as he has promised.

Here is the Advent truth: Before Christ comes in glory he comes to us in every moment of our existence. The question we must ask ourselves is whether we recognize him, welcome him, wait for him, yearn for him in all these moments? Or are we preoccupied with ourselves and all the passing pains and pleasures of life? Advent reminds us that we really don't have time to let ourselves be overly concerned with anything less than the coming of the Lord.

Watching can be understood in two ways. There is the watching that looks outward, to see the Lord coming through the door. And there is the watching that looks inward, to see within ourselves what obstacles stand in the way of our wholeheartedly receiving the Lord.

I read a beautiful fable [9] in which the Christ figure, a golden-haired boy named Gibbie, who is mute and also very poor, arrives at the cottage of an elderly couple who live at the edge of the great mountains, maybe at the edge of the world. Gibbie is welcomed with open arms by the wife, Janet. Janet has read one book, the Bible, over and over again for the past twenty or thirty years, and her whole life is focused on the coming of her Lord. She expects him every single day, and when she gets up in the morning it is to sweep the house, even the rafters of her poor thatched cottage, for his visit. The goodness and love of this woman, who is truly formed by the word of God, is a tremendous and appealing faith witness.

One sees clearly, however, that Janet welcomes Gibbie as she welcomes every person who crosses her threshold—as if that person were the Lord. Janet is always watching and always receiving the Lord.

Do we watch and wait for the Lord that acutely? Do we wake up every morning calling on Jesus to come that day? Do we sweep out of our hearts all gloomy, untrustful thoughts in preparation for his arrival?

That is the purpose of the Advent season. During these days before Christmas, each of us needs to slow down internally. We won't do any less work if our hearts are at peace and quiet. In fact, we may even do more and better work...but that's not the point.

The point of Advent is to remind ourselves to live with great singleness of purpose. The coming of Jesus is worth watching and waiting for.

Lord Jesus, help us to watch and wait for your coming at every moment with the same expectancy and desire as we would want to have in our final moment.

40

ACTIVE WAITING

The word of God came to John the son of Zechariah in the wilderness. He went into all the region around the Jordan, proclaiming a baptism of repentance for the forgiveness of sins.

LUKE 3:2-3

We have two witnesses who show us something about how to wait during Advent for the coming of the Lord. One is Saint John the Baptizer; the other is Mary, the mother of Jesus. Both of these holy people waited actively (not passively) for Jesus.

Saint Luke presents John as a *prophet:* "The word of God came to John." True prophets are those who hear the word of God and proclaim it, whatever the cost. When prophets speak the word they have heard, something happens in the hearts of those of us who listen. We hear and are overwhelmed by the truth. In a sense, the same fire enters into our hearts that is burning in those of the prophets, and we cry out almost in agony: What can we do? What does this word ask of me? We know we cannot remain the same; something must change in our life. But what, and how?

What did John say to us? He told us, "Prepare the way of the Lord, make his paths straight" (Luke 3:4). John waited for the Lord by preaching a baptism of repentance. He wanted us to live our normal lives, certainly, but he urged us to do it with justice. That means giving to everyone what is due: an honest wage or even an honest answer, for example. The word that John heard cannot remain in a heart where there is cheating or lying or violence of any kind against one's neighbor.

John sends those of us who have been converted right back to our own daily existence, but he doesn't mince words. Our lives must be different because of the word we have received. That word, for us as well as for the prophet himself, is both a gift and a responsibility.

And what of Mary, the mother of the Word Incarnate? Her waiting seems more private. She goes to be with her cousin, Elizabeth, who is pregnant with that same John who became the Baptizer. But how can we call Mary a witness when she speaks almost not at all, when the child she carries is mute, helpless, and defenseless within her womb? Does Mary show us the way to prepare for the Lord as the prophet John does?

Perhaps to hear the Word that Mary carries we must be mute ourselves. Maybe we must become helpless and defenseless ourselves before we can understand her message.

Each of us knows, in one way or another, how hard it is to accept being helpless. We want to make "it" happen, whatever "it" may be—even in "holy things," like experiencing God in prayer...or making the Lord Jesus come.

And in what sense are we to be defenseless? We all know how rare it is to find a person today who is not on guard, well-defended on every side, perhaps even emotionally walled up with a moat to keep out any unpleasant or hurtful invasion. Our defenses may be so strong that we cannot possibly hear the approach of the Savior, and so we will never leap for sheer joy (as John did in Elizabeth's womb) in the simple presence of the only one who can truly free us.

But Mary tells us by her example not to be afraid. She has been asked to do the impossible—

to give birth to God—but she accepts her mission in humility and faith. Like us, she awaits the coming of Jesus, but she does so by making the choice to be open and cooperate with the divine will.

Just as children do not realize how dependent they are on their mother until they grow up and see her from an adult perspective, I suspect we who belong to Christ are far more dependent on his mother than we can even imagine. When we are fully mature in Christ we will understand that Mary is always quietly there, showing us how to await her son.

And so we move along in our Advent journey, accompanied by these two very special witnesses, each encouraging us to wait actively for the Lord. John urges us to prepare the way of the Lord in the very midst of our daily activity; Mary simply carries the Word in her womb, showing by her example what being helpless and defenseless is really all about.

O Lord, with John may we prepare your way in our daily activities, and with Mary may we accept our vulnerability and let go of our defenses.

41

THE SPIRIT AND FIRE

"He will baptize you with the Holy Spirit and fire."

MATTHEW 3:11

To read the newspapers today—or just to talk with people—can be very depressing. There just aren't that many signs of harmony. Families are split, communities are divided within themselves, and nations seem to have nowhere near the kind of mutual respect and acceptance that is necessary for world peace.

But if our world seems cold and hard, we Christians believe that there is a fire that has been kindled that is the hope and sign of the messianic age. And it is burning here and now in our hearts.

Saint John the Baptizer speaks three times of fire. Twice he describes fire that will consume all that is not of the kingdom of God. It is the same fire that Saint John the Evangelist speaks of in his wonderful description of the vine and the branches: The branches that do not bear fruit "are gathered, thrown into the fire, and burned" (John 15:6).

But the Baptizer promises another fire: "I baptize you with water for repentance, but one who is more powerful than I is coming after me....He will baptize you with the Holy Spirit and fire" (Matthew 3:11).

The Holy Spirit is fire in the heart. Anyone who submits to this fire will never know the other fire, the consuming fire threatened for those who do not bear fruit. However, I think both fires are really the same. When we choose the fire, it purifies and transforms us. When we do not choose the fire, it consumes us.

The desire for God is the way this inner Spirit-fire expresses itself. All of us who are baptized into Christ carry within ourselves a flame of love. It is there whether we are aware of it or not, and it is always reaching out to spread itself to others.

The fire of the Spirit that is within us cannot be equated with natural fire and natural heat.

Maybe that is why many do not really believe in it. But have you ever felt a coldness and even hardness of heart toward someone, and then—after bringing that person into your heart in prayer—found your attitude much softened toward him or her? Can we not say that this softening, this melting of barriers, is the work of the Spirit's fire within us?

The Spirit we received at Baptism is ever within us: leveling the high places, smoothing the rough with a steady flame, transforming our hearts in readiness for the Lord's full and final coming. "If you will, you can become all flame" as one of the desert fathers challenged his disciple.

Let us allow the Spirit to melt away barriers of pride and fear, of seeing one another in competition with ourselves. It is one and the same Spirit burning within each of us. Let us be totally reconciled with one another: "Live in harmony with one another, in accordance with Christ Jesus" (Romans 15:5). *Then* we will be fit to glorify God with one heart and one voice.

This is truly to prepare the way of the Lord.

Spirit of Jesus, melt away all our defenses, that we may become all flame.

42

ACTIVE WATCHFULNESS

"He commands the doorkeeper to be on the watch. Therefore keep awake—for you do not know when the master of the house will come."

MARK 13:34-35

The key to understanding the prophetic exhortations of all Christian texts is *watchfulness*. Active watchfulness is one of the key Christian virtues. This awareness has a very important place in Christian spirituality. It is the basis of the daily office of vigils, which monks and many lay people pray every night. It encourages us to be ready and waiting—in the here and now—for the coming of the Lord. Watchfulness is also the root of the Christian tradition of praying over and over, "Come, Lord Jesus."

This same idea of living in the present moment is one of the key concepts of the spirituality developed by Alcoholics Anonymous (A.A.). *Today*—twenty-four hours—is the time span in which a recovering alcoholic lives and functions. Someone with the disease of alcoholism is advised not to promise never to take a drink again for the rest of his or her life. Instead, a recovering alcoholic is encouraged to stay sober for just one day at a time. That's all he or she asks God to give the strength for: one day of sobriety.

We all know about living in the past, but I would wager that each one of us is also very aware of our tendency to anticipate events or behaviors that have not yet taken place. In A.A. language, this is called *projection* (not the same as Jung's use of the term). Projection is reacting emotionally to (or fantasizing about) an event or behavior that has not happened yet. For example, if I make a decision as abbess and at the same time allow myself to feel anxious and depressed because "everyone in the community is going to dislike this decision and me for making it"—this is projection. The decision hasn't even been announced and I'm reacting emotionally to others' responses without giving them the trust and freedom and responsibility to respond well.

Projection is a terrible waste of energy, and it may also be a self-fulfilling prophecy. By expecting a poor response, I call forth the poor

response. How often do we live in such antici-
patory fear or depression? Sometimes we create
with our fantasizing all sorts of gruesome sce-
narios that will never even happen.

The fact is, we don't have the strength or
energy to live yesterday, today, and tomorrow at
the same time. Jesus said it best: "Today's troubles
are enough for today" (Matthew 6:34). We can
only be watchful for the Lord *now*. There is an
old Sanskrit proverb that goes something like
this: "Look to this day. For it is life. The very life
of life. In its brief course lie all."

If we truly live each day, without anticipat-
ing or projecting what is going to happen, life is
going to have many surprises for us and we will
surely be more happy. Active watchfulness is
possible only here and now.

Be alert, watch, and pray. Do not be anxious for yourself. Do not fear what might come.
False prophets will arise seeking to instill fear
and distrust of the future, but God is with us. If
there is confusion or misunderstanding, perse-
vere in charity and actively wait. Be watchful
today.

---

*Today is our now where we truly meet
you, O Lord. Turn away all those false
fears that steal present realities.*

43

THE DUTY OF DELIGHT

Sing for joy, O heavens, and exult, O earth; break forth, O mountains, into singing! For the Lord has comforted his people, and will have compassion on his suffering ones.

ISAIAH 49:13

Dorothy Day once wrote: "It is not always easy to be joyful, to keep in mind the duty of delight." When I watched a video recently, *The Long Journey to Guadalupe,* I noticed a striking contrast. In the faces of the older women and men on the screen there were the obvious lines of hardship and toil, but there was also a look of sheer joy and delight in their pilgrimage to pay homage to the Virgin Mary. They seemed to personify the description of the Israelites returning to Zion: "A highway shall be there, and it shall be called the Holy Way....The ransomed of the Lord shall return, and come to Zion with singing; everlasting joy shall be upon their heads; they shall obtain joy and gladness, and sorrow and sighing shall flee away" (Isaiah 35:8, 10).

When Mary revealed herself to the native people of Mexico as Our Lady of Guadalupe, she showed herself to be one of them—even in her facial appearance. But more than that, Mary put the indigenous people in touch with their own ancestral heritage and further still to the source and origin of all creation. They look into the face of their beloved "Guadalupana" and know that they are beloved children of God. If Mary loves them, why should they fear anything?

But then the pilgrims walk home, back into their hard life. And the rains don't come or the baby is very sick or the thousand other problems that are part of human existence recur. Then the Mexican pilgrims have to do what Dorothy Day is talking about. They have to "keep in mind the duty of delight." They have to touch their medal or plastic picture of Our Lady and remember what she told them: "I am a compassionate mother."

I received an e-mail from a friend whose mother-in-law's surgery went well. In this letter

186 SEASONS OF GRACE

the man mentions that several people wrote, assuring the family of their prayers but saying they were sorry that the illness was happening during the Christmas season. He responded in a way characteristic of him. He said that his family had felt surrounded and upheld by prayer, and he concluded: "Hey! Isn't that what the Christmas season is all about? God is with us in our lives—in our tragedies as well as in our wonderful celebrations. It's all one fabric."

I think he is right. The duty of delighting in Christmas is not contingent on human events. Our joy is based only on our being mindful of the deepest meaning of Christmas: God is with us—truly, in the flesh, for all time and in all circumstances.

Perhaps remembering this is most difficult for people who are not in extraordinary circumstances. We here at the abbey, for example, live a pretty ordinary, comfortable—albeit stretched at present—existence. We don't want to magnify our little aches and pains into tragedies. They are just normal, run-of-the-mill, human experiences of life. So how do we keep in mind our duty of delight? We do so by finding our *own* ways to see the faces of Jesus and his mother in the midst of our Christmas celebrations.

There's a story of a man who was lost in the woods, and he was very hungry. He finally came into a clearing where there was a house with a sign in the window: FRESH BREAD BAKED HERE DAILY. "Ah," he thought, "the end of my hunger!" He knocked on the door and asked the woman who answered, "Would you give me some bread?" She said, "Oh, we don't make bread here, we make only signs."

The point of this story for me is that we have to stay with the signs. The sign may be a slight injury to our pride or recognition for a job well done, a misunderstanding or a reconciliation, a mystical experience or a dark night of the soul. My advice to you is to stay with the sign until it becomes bread. Stay with the pain or the joy until the divine presence is revealed.

The lines on the faces of the Mexican peasants didn't happen overnight, nor did their simple and profound faith blossom in a moment. The duty of delight springs up out of a very deep place within us. We have to nurture it by remembering what is truly important in life.

Jesus and Mary, keep us faithful on the journey that brings us at last into the light. In this Christmas season, help us to keep in mind the duty of delight.

44

STAND AND WAIT

I waited patiently for the LORD; he inclined to me and heard my cry.

PSALM 40:1

Waiting can be a very humbling experience...if it doesn't first move us to anger. We all wait much of our lives, and most of the time we hate it. But perhaps waiting can be a very deep, spiritual activity. As T.S. Eliot wrote in his *Four Quartets:* "The faith and the love and the hope are all in the waiting." [10]

Contemplatives know that prayer can be primarily an experience of waiting. We pray to God and we wait—perhaps not experiencing much of anything for long periods of time. We have a terrible longing for something, a great gnawing hunger at the center of our being, but our experience has taught us that if we are seeking only ourselves or our own satisfaction in our prayer we will find only restlessness. So we pray, and we wait.

The early Christians were imbued with this stance towards God. They waited for the Lord with great eagerness, and—though they were certainly waiting for the expected second coming —their humble and faithful vigilance in waiting held more meaning than perhaps even they realized.

What is the posture of body that most often accompanies waiting? Not always, but very often, we wait standing. There is a meaning in standing and a way to stand that is important to our prayer life.

When we stand we express our rootedness in the earth, our very "creatureliness." If we stand correctly—that is, not slouching over or leaning against something, but with our weight evenly distributed on our two feet—there is a balance and flow of energy in the same way as when we sit or kneel straight in good prayer posture. When we stand we are at attention, so to speak. We are ready for action.

Romano Guardini says that kneeling is the side of worship in rest and quietness and standing is the side of vigilance and action. It is the respect of the servant in attendance, of the soldier on duty.

The early Christians stood when they prayed. The *orante* or praying person in the familiar catacomb representation stands in the long flowing robes of a woman of rank. She prays with outstretched hands, in perfect freedom and obedience, awaiting the word, ready to perform it with joy.

Standing during the liturgy is not simply a matter of taking a break between kneeling and sitting. It is a sacred sign of our attentiveness to the word of God, our readiness to do that word, our willingness to accept our own emptiness and neediness, our waiting for the Lord.

Let us become aware of all the waiting spaces in our lives, whether they be in a checkout line or a chapel. Let us not be tempted to fill every moment so we don't have to experience the *awfulness* of waiting. Rather, let us stand and wait in hope with the early Christians for the coming of the Lord.

Lord, the faith and the love and the hope are in the waiting. May we meet you there.

45

MARY'S GIFT

"Whoever does the will of God is my brother and sister and mother."

MARK 3:35

Bow down before God's temple, for it is holy. The point of the Church's doctrine of the Immaculate Conception is that we recognize the uniqueness of Mary in the human race. It is fitting, the Church says, that she who is so closely related to the God-man Jesus—his own mother—should have been free from sin from the moment of her conception.

In a certain sense, this sinlessness separates Mary from us. Every other person who has come into the world has sin except the one for whom we all wait...and his mother. But in the course of Mary's life, this gift was totally concealed. What strikes us instead when we read the Scriptures is that Mary's life was marked by suffering, misunderstanding, pain—just like ours. In her sinlessness Mary is removed from us, but in her anxiety and confusion she is wholly like us.

Sometimes the gifts of God are covered very well. Sometimes even a person himself or herself does not fathom the gifts of grace God has bestowed. For example, from the divine vantage point Mary is whole, beautiful, a flawless image of God's own life. From the vantage point of her contemporaries, however, Mary was poor, unfortunate, even an object of pity. God's gift within Mary was hidden indeed. God's gifts within you and me are also hidden.

A contemplative is one who *sees* and *loves*. Look and truly see the sinlessness in Mary—and love it. Look and truly see the beauty of God in others—and love it. Look and truly see the beauty of God within yourself—and know the real mystery: that we, too, bear within us the divine image that was Mary's from the moment of her conception. Bow down before God's temple, for it is holy.

Lord Jesus, keep us faithful in doing the will of God, so that we, too, may bear the divine image more fully.

46

CHRISTMAS EVE

In the beginning was the Word, and the Word was with God, and the Word was God.... And the Word became flesh and lived among us.

JOHN 1:1, 14

Today the mystery is accomplished. For four weeks all who believe the word of God have been pressing towards this day, waiting with watchful hope, with the flame of our desire growing brighter each week. And now the mystery is upon us.

I don't want to multiply words that might obscure the mystery. Let it touch you where you are right now. Because that is what the Incarnation is all about.

The Incarnation means that the infinite love, wisdom, and power of God simply could not contain itself; it had to become flesh as we are flesh, so that all creation could know its God firsthand and not by hearsay or imagination.

The mystery of the Incarnation is so great that many have found it as much a scandal and stumbling block as the Cross. The Arian heresy, which denies the divinity of Jesus, is still alive today, although most of us do not recognize it. A prominent American theologian has written that it is simply impossible to believe that God should become a human being. (Sometimes we can learn more about what we believe from those who question or doubt that belief.)

Yes, the Incarnation is literally incredible. We can't understand logically what it could possibly mean for the transcendent to become tangible. But we can yield in faith to the mystery, and in so doing we can let love incarnate touch our lives in the here and now.

We can open our entire being to the Word made flesh because the Word has truly become one with human life. Nothing that is human is foreign to Jesus, the son of Mary but also the Son of God. Saint Irenaeus said that what has not been fully assumed could never have been fully healed, meaning that our salvation could not be complete unless Christ was truly flesh of our flesh.

O Christian, know your dignity this night! God has come into the world as a little child. Let the mystery touch you.

Father, may we yield in faith to the mystery of Christmas.

47

CELEBRATE PEACE

"Glory to God in the highest heaven, and on earth peace among those whom he favors."

The first acclamation to greet God-made-flesh was a song of angels: "Glory to God in the highest heaven, and on earth peace among those whom he favors."

In the two thousand years since that glorious event, however, the search for the fullness of peace goes on, and we long for the promised day when peace will reign over all the earth. For only on that day will we humans be able to send back to heaven the song that now only angels can truly sing.

Pope John Paul II, in his World Day of Peace message in 1986, made a strong appeal to all of us to reflect on peace and to celebrate peace. He wrote that to celebrate peace in the midst of difficulties—such as those of today—is to proclaim our trust in humanity.

We Christians need to *celebrate* peace. It is not enough to *pray* for peace as though it were an unknown commodity—something out there that we want to lay hold of. No, we must taste and savor the peace that we already know—the peace that is already evident in certain people, families, communities. And if we want peace we must do the things that make for peace.

In his message to the world, John Paul described two keys to peace today: human solidarity and development. We are all part of the human family, simply by being born into this world. "Our common bonds of humanity," John Paul wrote, "demand that we live in harmony and that we promote what is good for one another." [11] Solidarity and development are basic keys to peace because if we believe that we all share a single human existence then we must act differently towards one another and promote what is good for others.

The Rule of St. Benedict says that the sisters and brothers should anticipate the needs of others and do what will benefit the other rather than what will benefit themselves. Saint Paul urges us to "Do nothing from selfish ambition or conceit, but in humility regard others as better than yourselves. Let each of you look not to your own interests, but to the interests of others" (Philippians 2:3-4). And a Hindu master once said that every time we put ourselves first we are making war.

When we learn to live for our family, our friends, our country, our world, then—and only then—will there will be peace on earth.

Lord Jesus, we celebrate the peace that you give when we realize our true solidarity with all people. We commit ourselves to live in such a way that promotes the development of others.

48

OUR SOURCE OF UNITY

*"May they all be one. As you, Father,
are in me and I am in you, may they
also be in us, so that the world may believe that you have sent me."*

JOHN 17:21

It was on January 25th (the last day of the
Unity Octave) in 1959 that Pope John XXIII announced the twenty-first Ecumenical Council. If
you are like me, then you may have forgotten,
as I did, that this is its proper title. We have become more used to calling it Vatican II or the
Second Vatican Council, but it was first and foremost an *Ecumenical* Council.

In his comments on January 25th, Pope John
said that the Council would be not only for the

spiritual good and joy of the Roman Catholic Church. He desired to invite the other Christian communions to seek again that "unity...to which so many souls aspire from all corners of the earth." [12]

Pope John's vision was that the Catholic Church *first* had to renew herself, but then she had to be ready to enter into deeper communion with our "separated brethren." In the Decree on Ecumenism that came out of the council, there is this striking sentence: "There can be no ecumenism worthy of the name without a change of heart. For it is from newness of attitudes (cf. Ephesians 4:23), from self-denial and unstinted love, that yearnings for unity take their rise and grow toward maturity." [13]

To me this insight is remarkable! When we read Christ's own prayer for unity, we realize that he understood even before he left his disciples that they would be tempted to split with one another over trivial things. He knew that unity is difficult to maintain, and so he did two things. First, he prayed for us, that we would remain *one* with one another, and second, he pointed out that the source of our unity is our union with him and his union with the Father: "May they all be one. As you, Father, are in me and I am in you, may they also be in us, so that the world may believe that you have sent me."

Christian unity does not happen automatically or easily. We need to long for it and work for it, but we must always remember the source of our unity. As the decree puts it: "They can achieve depth and ease in strengthening mutual brotherhood to the degree that they enjoy profound communion with the Father, the Word, and the Spirit." [14]

Jesus, may the pain of our separation from one another enter into our hearts. Open all of us to the healing work of your Spirit.

49

THE MEANING OF SUFFERING

Abraham took the wood of the burnt of-
fering and laid it on his son Isaac, and
he himself carried the fire and the knife.
So the two of them walked on together.
Isaac said to his father Abraham, "Fa-
ther!" And he said, "Here I am, my son."
He said, "The fire and the wood are
here, but where is the lamb for a burnt
offering?" Abraham said, "God himself
will provide the lamb for a burnt offer-
ing, my son." So the two of them walked
on together. When they came to the place
that God had shown him, Abraham
built an altar there and laid the wood
in order. He bound his son Isaac, and
laid him on the altar, on top of the wood.
Then Abraham reached out his hand
and took the knife to kill his son. But

the angel of the Lord called to him from heaven, and said, "Abraham, Abraham!" And he said, "Here I am." He said, "Do not lay your hand on the boy or do anything to him; for now I know that you fear God, since you have not withheld your son, your only son, from me." And Abraham looked up and saw a ram, caught in a thicket by its horns. Abraham went and took the ram and offered it up as a burnt offering instead of his son. So Abraham called that place "The Lord will provide" as it is said to this day, "On the mount of the Lord it shall be provided."

GENESIS 22:6-14

God and Abraham are rather extraordinary portraits of two fathers (if we can talk about both of them as fathers in the same breath). But isn't it striking? Both of these fathers have a beloved only son. And both of these fathers are ready to sacrifice their boy for a greater good.

Here we also have two sons: Isaac, a youth, and Jesus, a man in his prime. Both are on a journey that will lead ultimately to their executions; both will carry on their backs the wood for the sacrifice; both are ready—young Isaac in innocence and unquestioning trust in his father, Jesus in his absolute surrender to his Father.

There is one very big difference between these two stories, however. An angel of the Lord appears from nowhere to stay the hand of Abraham and Isaac is spared. His life was needful for the fulfillment of a promise. Jesus, on the other hand, was not spared, even though he told his disciples, "Do you think that I cannot appeal to my Father, and he will at once send me more than twelve legions of angels?" (Matthew 26:53). But Jesus knew that his death was needful for the fulfillment of the promise of salvation: "But how then would the scriptures be fulfilled, which say it must happen in this way?" (Matthew 26: 54).

I wonder what Jesus' own thoughts were when he was a young boy studying the Hebrew scriptures and listening to the story of Abraham and Isaac read in the synagogue on the Sabbath. Did he have some inkling that this story was not so much history as prophecy? Did he suspect that somehow his own destiny was intimately connected with that of Isaac, the beloved son of Abraham, and with his sacrifice? And most of all did he believe that an angel would come again to free the beloved son and replace him with a ram? We really don't know the answer to these questions. The Gospels don't give us a clue, because Jesus never publicly identified himself with Isaac.

But there is another beloved son with whom Jesus does identify himself, and that is the Suffering Servant of Isaiah. There is one aspect of this person as Isaiah portrays him that can help us to enter more fully into the meaning of Jesus' passion and death *and* our own personal suffering.

According to biblical scholars, Jesus drew upon the traditional image of the Suffering Servant to understand his own destiny. It was Isaiah's concept of suffering that atoned for the sins of others that Jesus carried to its logical conclusion. In the time of Jesus, sincere Jews asked the questions that we are still asking today: Since it is obvious that innocent people suffer as much as the guilty, we cannot link suffering with punishment for sins. But could the opposite be true? Could it be that the death of an innocent person can atone for the sins of others? Is it possible that the noble suffering of one person somehow heals the afflictions of others?

It was this very belief in atonement in the midst of absurd suffering that inspired Isaiah's hymns—and Jesus applied this understanding to himself. There are several indications in the Gospels, especially in the conversation at the Last Supper and in the predictions of the passion uttered on the way to Jerusalem. But one strong reference to *atoning* suffering is in the Gospel of Mark. When James and John request positions of power in the Kingdom, Jesus reveals his own understanding of his mission and of his death: "The Son of Man came not to be served but to serve, and to give his life as a ransom for many" (Mark 10:45).

This echoes the experience of the Suffering Servant: "He was wounded for our transgressions, crushed for our iniquities; upon him was the punishment that made us whole" (Isaiah 53:5). The Servant's death is "an offering for sin" (Isaiah 53:10). The sufferings of the innocent servant would atone for the sins of many.

Here is the only way Christians can understand the suffering of Jesus and our own suffering or that of others: Individual suffering does not end with the individual. A suffering person is truly a cooperator in the transformation of human suffering.

There was a Congress on Suffering not too long ago attended by men and women who had endured tremendous physical and emotional pain (especially in prison camps and torture chambers), and also by persons who were currently suffering. I'd like to quote a few remarks from these people.

A theologian who was a dialysis patient and died shortly after the Congress said: "The problem of suffering rises from the mere fact that humans never resign themselves to the inevitability of suffering in their own lives and those of others near and dear to them."

Another theologian (from Harvard) who was also suffering from a fatal illness and died soon after the Congress said: "Love your enemy, turn your cheek to receive the blows of others, have compassion, and accompany those who suffer even into their sufferings...as Jesus truly joined us in our agonies. In his passion Jesus exhibited what compassion, or suffering with, really means."

What we need to remember is that Jesus was not a victim of circumstances. He freely chose to enter into the suffering that his teaching and beliefs brought upon him. He knew from his *biblical faith* (which we all share) that suffering freely accepted somehow heals and saves.

God will ask each of us to sacrifice our "Isaac." We don't know what the specific sacrifice will be—perhaps no more than an occupation we love or a house we've grown accustomed to. Or perhaps we will be asked to sacrifice our very idea of holiness and how it should look in us. Surely for each of us at some time in our lives, we will be asked to sacrifice our robust health and energy. Finally, we will be asked to accept the deaths of our loved ones and eventually our own.

We don't know our "Isaac," and neither do we know if an angel will come at the last minute to replace our sacrifice. But we do know that Jesus yielded to suffering and entered into healing and life for many, and so can we.

Lord Jesus, may we follow your example of yielding to suffering so that we may enter into the fullness of life with you.

50

WE ARE ON THE WAY TOGETHER

If then there is any encouragement in Christ, any consolation from love, any sharing in the Spirit, any compassion and sympathy, make my joy complete: be of the same mind, having the same love, being in full accord and of one mind.

PHILIPPIANS 2:1-2

We Christians are "on the way" together, moving towards that purity of heart which is necessary in order to be able to see God in glory. We do this simply by choosing to be with one another in community—in our joys as well as in our sorrows.

Thomas Merton, in a talk on "Life and Community" defines community as being "Wherever you knock up against somebody in pursuit of doing something together." [15] This doesn't sound too romantic, and that's the point. Community isn't romantic. It's earthy and material and messy and ordinary. Community is simply being with one another intentionally.

God chooses whom we knock up against, whose sufferings and joys we are asked to share. But we freely choose whether or not to be in community in the midst of all that knocking about. Whether it be a monastery, a parish, a workplace, a neighborhood, or even a family, we *make* community, we *build* community, we *foster* community.

To be with others in their moments of greatest joy or suffering is a great privilege. It is the way we touch others at the most intimate—the most mystical—points of their lives, the points at which the action of God is most palpable. At any given moment in a community, one or more of us is experiencing this "moment of truth." To be with others—to support, accept, and love them—in these moments is the meaning of community itself.

Here are some beatitudes for community life: Blessed is the community that laughs together easily. Blessed is the community that bears sorrow together sympathetically. Blessed is the community that can be silent together without un-easiness. Blessed is the community whose members share common goals and—without fear of recrimination—challenge one another to achieve those goals. Blessed is the community in which each individual is respected and loved in his or her uniqueness and in which each member is involved personally in the life of the whole.

God truly blesses our many communities, so let's continue to choose simply to be with one another in our joys and in our sorrows as we continue on our way together.

Jesus, you who are our way, continue to travel with us in community so that in the midst of our sorrows and joys we may recognize God's hidden glory.

NOTES

1. André Chouraqui, "The Psalms" in *Liturgy O.C.S.O.,* volume 13 (February 1979), 3-36.

2. Lawrence Martin Jenco, O.S.M., *Bound to Forgive: The Pilgrimage to Reconciliation of a Beirut Hostage* (Notre Dame, Indiana: Ave Maria Press, 1995), 13-14.

3. Josef Stierli, "The Development of the Church's Devotion to the Sacred Heart in Modern Times" in *Heart of the Saviour: A Symposium on Devotion to the Sacred Heart,* edited by Josef Stierli (New York: Herder and Herder, 1958), 117.

4. Otto F. Bond, ed., *Première Étape: Basic French Readings* (Boston: D.C. Heath and Company, 1961).

5. Bernard of Clairvaux, *Sermon 83 on the Song of Songs* in Cistercian Fathers Series, Vol. 40 (Kalamazoo, Michigan: Cistercian Publications, 1980).

6. J.D. Salinger, *Franny and Zooey* (New York: Bantam, 1961), 196.

7. Rainer Maria Rilke, *Letters to a Young Poet* (New York: W.W. Norton & Co., 1934), 59.

8. Kahil Gibran, *The Prophet* (New York: Alfred A. Knopf, 1973), 29.

9. George MacDonald, *The Baronet's Song* (Minneapolis: Bethany House Publishers, 1983).

10. T.S. Eliot, "Four Quartets" in *The Complete Poems and Plays 1909-1950* (New York: Harcourt, Brace & World, Inc., 1952) 126-127.

11. Pope John Paul II, World Day of Peace message, 1986.

12. Pope John XXIII, "Announcement of Ecumenical Council and Roman Synod," January 25, 1959 in *The Pope Speaks,* volume 5 (Autumn 1959), 401.

13. "Decree on Ecumenism" in *The Documents of Vatican II,* Walter M. Abbott, S.J., ed. (New York: Herder and Herder, 1966) 351.

14. Ibid.

15. Thomas Merton, talk titled "Life and Community," Electronic Paperbacks, 1976 (Chappaqua, New York, TM-11).